Praise for *How to Make Money with Social Media, Second Edition*

"Whoever says you can't make money with social media clearly has not read this book. Not only is social media marketing profitable, it is the great equalizer, allowing small businesses to compete against giants. Read this book and start taking your business to the next level."

—**Michael Stelzner,** Author, *Launch*, and Founder, SocialMediaExaminer.com

"Believe it or not, there are many ways to make money, both directly and indirectly, through social media. The problem is that most people are doing it [social media] wrong. This book shows you the right way to go to market with a social media strategy."

—**Joe Pulizzi,** Author, *Epic Content Marketing*, and Founder, Content Marketing Institute

"Many doubt the ROI of Social Media. Turner and Shah silence this doubt with cold hard facts."

—**Erik Qualman,** Author, *What Happens in Vegas Stays on YouTube*

"If you're not making money through social media you are missing a golden opportunity, and this book unlocks that opportunity."

—**Ian Cleary,** Founder, Razor Social

"I'm often asked by people if they could only buy one social media book which one should it be—and my answer is always *How to Make Money with Social Media*. Even now this is the most dog-eared, bookmarked, and sticky-noted social media book on my shelf!"

—**Viveka von Rosen,** Founder, LinkedIn into Business, and Author, *LinkedIn Marketing: An Hour a Day*

"Where's the ROI in social media? It's in Turner and Shah's book *How to Make Money with Social Media*!"

—**Lon Safko,** Author, *The Social Media Bible* and *The Fusion Marketing Bible*

"Do you want to finally learn how to make money with social media? Jamie Turner and Reshma Shah invite you to reframe your thinking about how social media can really work for your business. With concrete examples on how big businesses have set up their campaigns and step-by-step processes you can easily implement, you are guaranteed to take away some money-making ideas from this book. Fantastic!"

—**Andrea Vahl,** Co-Author of *Facebook Marketing All-in-One for Dummies*

"I've met an awful lot of social media experts in my career, and very few of them had the expertise and experience necessary to help people generate a positive ROI with their social media marketing efforts. If you're looking for a book that talks about real results, real case studies, and real techniques, read this book by Jamie Turner and Reshma Shah."

—**Emeric Ernoult,** CEO, AgoraPulse

"The next evolution in social media marketing is closing the loop by tracking and adjusting your efforts so your business can make a difference in the world. Read this book. It will point you in the right direction and teach you how to make money using today's marketing structures."

—**Phyllis Khare,** Co-Founder, Social Media Manager School, and creator of TimeBliss.ME

"Social media is important whether you're a local company or a global one. This book shows you how to launch a successful campaign whether it's in your neighborhood or around the globe."

—**Ulrich Henes,** Executive Producer, Brand2Global Conferences

"Turner and Shah have once again perfectly captured the whats, wheres, and whys of social media. In this highly readable book, they cut right to what matters most and deliver a powerful case for real-world, pragmatic social media interaction."

—**Tad DeWree**, Principal, Essential Branding, and Author, *50 Essential Rules of Great Branding*

"If you're ready to take your social media campaigns to the next level, read this book. It provides a step-by-step plan on how to generate real results and a positive ROI."

—**Ahmed Sabry,** CEO, Digital Marketing Arts

Praise for the Previous Edition of
How to Make Money with Social Media

"Return on investment in social media is like the weather: Everybody talks about it, but nobody is doing anything about it. With this book, Jamie Turner and Reshma Shah set you up for success with some key fundamentals, and then give you some very specific and illustrative examples on how to calculate the ROI of your social media efforts."

—**Scott Monty,** Global Digital Communications, Ford Motor Company

"Social media isn't a fad. It's not going away. This book adds tools to your thinking on the matter."

—**Chris Brogan,** *New York Times* bestselling Co-Author, *Trust Agents*, and Publisher, chrisbrogan.com

"*How to Make Money with Social Media* is a very practical, user-friendly book on how to use social media for brand building. It is comprehensive, yet conversational, and a joy to read!"

—**Jag Sheth,** Professor of Marketing, Emory University

"There are a lot of reasons I like this book, but I'll give you just two now: First, I like its no-nonsense approach to connect social media and your business goals. And second, it doesn't toss around too many ridiculous acronyms, jargon, or business-speak (which is a pet peeve of mine). Instead, it's written in an accessible voice and engaging style."

—**Ann Handley,** Chief Content Officer, MarketingProfs, and Co-Author, *Content Rules: How to Create Killer Blogs, Podcasts, Videos, Ebooks, Webinars (and More) That Engage Customers and Ignite Your Business*

How to Make Money with Social Media

HOW TO MAKE MONEY WITH SOCIAL MEDIA

An Insider's Guide to Using New and Emerging Media to Grow Your Business

Second Edition

Jamie Turner
Reshma Shah

Associate Publisher: Amy Neidlinger
Operations Specialist: Jodi Kemper
Cover Designer: Chuti Prasertsith
Managing Editor: Kristy Hart
Project Editor: Elaine Wiley
Copy Editor: Bart Reed
Proofreader: Sarah Kearns
Indexer: Tim Wright
Compositor: Nonie Ratcliff
Manufacturing Buyer: Dan Uhrig

Upper Saddle River, New Jersey 07458

For information about buying this title in bulk quantities, or for special sales opportunities (which may include electronic versions; custom cover designs; and content particular to your business, training goals, marketing focus, or branding interests), please contact our corporate sales department at corpsales@pearsoned.com or (800)382-3419.

For government sales inquiries, please contact governmentsales@pearsoned.com.

For questions about sales outside the U.S., please contact international@pearsoned.com.

Company and product names mentioned herein are the trademarks or registered trademarks of their respective owners.

Printed in the United States of America

First Printing August 2014

ISBN-10: 0-13-388833-9
ISBN-13: 978-0-13-388833-1

Pearson Education LTD.
Pearson Education Australia PTY, Limited.
Pearson Education Singapore, Pte. Ltd.
Pearson Education Asia, Ltd.
Pearson Education Canada, Ltd.
Pearson Educación de Mexico, S.A. de C.V.
Pearson Education—Japan
Pearson Education Malaysia, Pte. Ltd.

Library of Congress Control Number: 2014940712

To my wife, Dayna, who means the world to me. And to my children, McKensie, Grace, and Lily, who, for years, have put up with all my "wise" sayings.

—Jamie Turner

To my wonderfully supportive husband, Hitesh Shah, and my darling daughters, Maya and Anya. Thank you for the time away.

—Reshma Shah

Contents

Acknowledgments

Okay, this is strange. Here you are, holding this book in your hands, and you've decided to read the Acknowledgments section instead of reading the scintillating content in each and every page of this amazing masterpiece.

That means you're either standing in a bookstore waiting for a friend, or you're hoping we remembered to include your name somewhere in the upcoming paragraphs.

Well, this may come as a surprise to you, but what you're reading is actually the most important section of the book. We're not kidding. After all, writing a book is an amazingly collaborative process. Even though we're the ones who get our names on the cover, this book was written, rewritten, rewritten (again!), and then rewritten one more time, all with the help of a wide variety of people. And that was before it even got to the editors, which either means we're terrible writers (entirely possible, by the way) or that we had amazing amounts of great advice and help from our friends, family, and business associates.

With that in mind, we'd like to honor all those who were responsible for this book. Each and every one of you has helped in ways we can never repay. (And, oh, by the way, we're serious when we say we can never repay you. You aren't getting a dime. And, Mom, that includes you.)

We'd like to thank the following people: Amy Neidlinger, Tad DeWree with Mind4Marketing, Samantha Gale, Devna Thapliyal, Silvia Driver, Jennifer Simon, Brent Kuhn, Maribett Varner, Virginia Doty, Mike Turner, Jr., Nanci Steveson, JoAnn Sciarrino-Goggel, Rupal Mamtani, Guy Powell, Karri Hobson-Pape, the volunteers at ASchoolBell Rings.org and Kids4Kids360.org, GMSC students, and the Beatles (for singing primarily about love and peace).

We'd also like to thank our parents, Dr. Jagdish and Madhu Sheth, as well as Mike and Liz Turner.

Finally, we'd like to thank our friends at Pearson who have been inspirational throughout. They include Amy Neidlinger (again), Elaine Wiley, Chuti Prasertsith, Kristy Hart, Nonie Ratcliff, Dan Uhrig, and last but not least, Bart Reed.

Thank you all so much. Seriously, this wouldn't have happened without you.

About the Authors

Jamie Turner is an internationally recognized marketing expert and author who has helped The Coca-Cola Company, AT&T, CNN, and other global brands tackle complex business problems. He is the CEO of 60 Second Communications, a full-service marketing agency working with Samsung, The Coca-Cola Company, InterContinental Hotels Group, and others. He is also the founder of 60SecondMarketer.com, an online magazine that provides tips and techniques for marketers around the globe. He has been profiled in the world's best-selling marketing textbook, is a regular guest on CNN and HLN, and is a keynote speaker at events, trade shows, and corporations around the globe.

Reshma Shah, Ph.D. is an Assistant Professor in the Practice of Marketing at Goizueta Business School of Emory University. She is also a founder and partner at Inflexion Point Marketing Group. Dr. Shah's marketing insights and strategies have helped companies such as Ciba Vision, GE, IBM, Turner, The Coca-Cola Company, and UPS, among many others, improve their marketing return on investment. Her articles have appeared in several academic journals in the areas of marketing alliances and brand extensions. Dr. Shah was also the recipient of the Distinguished Educator Award at Emory University.

Mr. Turner and Dr. Shah are also cofounders of ASchoolBellRings.org, a nonprofit that builds schools and educational programs for impoverished children around the globe.

Introduction

If you're like a lot of people, you probably have some questions about social media. You may be asking whether social media is overhyped, whether something else will replace it, or whether it's just a big, fat waste of time.

But the important questions is, "Can I make money with social media?" After all, what's the point of setting up, launching, and running a social media campaign if it's not going to make money?

Well, we've got some good news. You *can* make money with social media—if you follow the right plan. The problem is that many people think that simply updating a Facebook page or uploading a YouTube video is a social media campaign.

It's not.

A well-run social media campaign is a program that's well thought out, well executed, and well managed. It's set up with a clear set of objectives, strategies, and tactics. Most importantly, it's designed to ultimately accomplish one thing: to generate revenue. Everything else is just a stop along the way.

Maybe you're thinking, "I'm just a small business owner, and all of my time goes into running my business. How can I possibly make the time to learn and use social media?" We can tell you from our own experience that social media doesn't have to be time consuming, especially if you set it up properly from the start.

Or you might be thinking, "I run a huge division of a large global organization. I just need to hire the right people to do my social media." But you can't *delegate* social media until you *understand* social media. And we're here to help you do exactly that.

You might even be thinking, "I work in a business-to-business company where it's all about requests for proposals (RFPs) and low price. Social media doesn't have a place in our company." We're here to tell you that social media isn't just for business-to-consumer companies. In fact, social media can be an extremely effective sales tool for business-to-business companies, too.

If you picked up this book looking for an encyclopedia of marketing theory, this might not be the book for you. If you picked it up looking for a simple introduction to the basics of social media, it might not be the book for you, either. But if you're looking for a book that will give you a practical roadmap designed to help you set up, launch, and run a money-making social media campaign, this could be just what you're looking for.

A Few Tips on Using This Book

We've divided the book into several segments that explore concepts such as the social media landscape, how to get set up for success, different social media platforms, how to integrate social media into your marketing plan, and how to measure social media. All these sections are designed to give you a practical roadmap to help you get going with a successful social media campaign.

We've also included a variety of callout boxes to highlight key ideas in the book. Sometimes you'll see boxes that read "The Big Idea"; other times you'll see boxes titled "Did You Know?" And still other times you'll see boxes titled "Money-Making Tip." They're all designed to help frame some of the issues in that section of the book.

You'll also see a number of references to additional content located on the 60 Second Marketer website. The 60 Second Marketer is an online magazine read by tens of thousands of marketing professionals around the globe each month. We've included several additional pages on the website that expand on topics covered in the book.

Finally, you'll notice that we end each chapter with key concepts and action steps designed to recap the chapter and review the specific steps to take based on those concepts. The key concepts and action steps aren't there just for grins—use them!

Okay, we've covered a lot of ground here. You're probably eager to get going.

You ready? We are, too. Just turn the page and we'll get started.

1

In the Beginning

Not long after the South by Southwest conference, Ricardo Guerrero had an idea that would change social media forever.

The date was Sunday, April 22, 2007 and Guerrero was relaxing with the latest edition of *The New York Times*. He was reading an article about Jack Dorsey and Biz Stone, the two inventors of a new social media platform called Twitter.

Guerrero had first learned about Twitter the previous month at South by Southwest, where it won the "Best of the Web" award. At the time, Twitter only had 100,000 users, and the future of the platform was still very much in doubt, so Guerrero was viewing it as a possible fad. But there was something about the platform that intrigued him, which is why he began trying to wrap his mind around a business application for it.

A lot has changed since that day in April 2007—the most important thing being that people have grown much more comfortable using tools such as Twitter, Pinterest, Facebook, Instagram, Google+, LinkedIn, and others as a way to connect with friends, business associates, and the brands they love.

But one fact hasn't changed: Businesses are still trying to figure out how best to use social media to generate revenue. Even though 77 percent of the Fortune 500 use social media for business,[1] only 12 percent of all businesses in the U.S. can tie their social media campaigns to revenue.[2]

That's exactly the challenge Ricardo Guerrero was facing when he was reading the article in *The New York Times*. Ricardo was a Web Strategist for Dell Computers in Austin, Texas, and was trying to figure out ways to turn followers into dollars. At the time, nobody really knew how to do it. In fact, social media was so new that one well-respected expert said calculating the ROI of a social media campaign was like trying to calculate the ROI of the office landscaping—no matter how hard you try, it can't accurately be done.[3]

But that answer didn't sit well with Ricardo. After all, if a company invests in a new technology, it should expect a return on its investment; otherwise, there's no reason to spend the money in the first place. It doesn't matter if you're a business owner, a marketing director, or a chief financial officer—if you spend money on any technology or piece of equipment, the reason you invest is because it will a) increase revenues, b) reduce costs, or c) improve efficiencies. If it can't do one of those three things, why invest in it at all?

So Ricardo was trying to figure out a way to use this new tool to help Dell increase revenues. Most people understood that Twitter and other tools like it could be used to grow brand awareness, but nobody had really figured out how to use social media to specifically grow revenues.

But then, not long after reading the article, the light bulb went off.

Why not build a massive Twitter following for Dell Outlet and drive leads to their e-commerce pages via Twitter? If you could build a big audience, then you could alert the followers to special discounts available only on the Dell Outlet web page. When the followers saw the tweets with the special discounts, a certain percentage would click through to learn more about the offer. A certain percentage of those who clicked from the tweet to the e-commerce page would become customers.

It seemed logical enough. After all, the direct marketing industry had been using similar methodologies for over 50 years. Their approach was to send a direct mail letter to, say, 100,000 people. Of the 100,000 people who received the direct mail letter, about 0.5 percent would order the product and become customers. If the revenue generated from those 500 new customers covered the cost of the marketing campaign plus the cost of other items (materials, overhead, labor, and so on), then you'd have a winning campaign. Ideally, there was a profit margin built into the calculation. If your campaign paid for all your costs *and* generated a profit, you could ramp up the campaign and grow revenues, in theory, indefinitely.

The question for Ricardo was how to use that kind of math and apply it to Twitter. The starting point would have to be to get enough followers to gain traction, but nobody knew what that magic number of followers was. What they *did* know was that most of the people on Twitter at the time were early adopters, and early adopters were exactly the kind of people who would be interested in discounts on Dell computers.

So, on June 5, 2007, Dell Outlet sent out its first tweet, which was a nonpromotional message designed to engage the handful of people who were following them at the time. About 12 months later, they had 1,000 followers, which is not a lot, but it was enough to generate $500,000 in revenue directly tied to the @DellOutlet Twitter account.[4] In other words, Dell generated an extra $500,000 in sales by being one of the first companies to figure out how to use a social media platform to drive prospects to an e-commerce page and convert them to customers.

It didn't take long for Guerrero and the rest of the Dell Outlet team to figure out they were on to something. By December, 2008, Dell had 2,500 Twitter followers and $1 million in sales tied to the Twitter account.

Over time, the Twitter following for Dell Outlet grew exponentially. By December 2009, they had nearly 1.5 million Twitter followers and had been the starting point for more than $6.5 million in sales across all Dell Twitter accounts.[5] Eventually, the Dell Outlet model got so much attention that other businesses jumped on the Twitter bandwagon and started using it as a revenue-generation tool as well.

But direct revenue generation only tells part of the Dell Outlet story. Although the $6.5 million in revenue was a huge success (especially when you consider that the cost of running the Dell Outlet Twitter account couldn't have been all *that* expensive), other factors should be taken into consideration. For example, a community of Dell fans were so enthralled with the special offers Dell Outlet was making via Twitter that they started to collect and share the coupons on the Dell Outlet Facebook page. This not only broadened the Dell fan base and promoted the Dell brand, it also drove additional prospects to the Dell Outlet e-commerce pages *at zero extra cost to Dell.* In other words, the Dell Outlet Facebook community was acting as an extra marketing department for the company, so for every $1 Dell Outlet spent on marketing, the online community was adding another 5¢, 10¢, or 15¢ to the equation.

All this begs the question: If the model for growing revenues with social media was established in 2007, why do only 12 percent of the companies using social media tie their efforts to revenue generation? Why don't 100 percent of the companies track their campaigns so that they can show the chief financial officer that $1 spent in social media generates $2 or $5 or $10 for their company?

The answer is simple—they don't know how to do it. Oh, sure, they know the *theory* of how to do it, but they don't know the specific steps involved in creating a social media campaign *that actually generates revenue.*

TOOLS, TIPS, AND TECHNIQUES

We like to measure what's easy to measure (likes, traffic, followers, bounce rates, etc.). The problem is that these are imperfect metrics because they don't indicate whether your campaign is actually generating revenue for your business. In order to grow your business with social media, you'll need to combine these metrics with additional formulas to calculate whether or not your campaign is working. You'll learn more about these important concepts in the upcoming chapters.

Another issue facing many people in charge of their social media campaigns is that *some social media campaigns aren't actually designed to generate revenue.*

Yes, you read that right. This is a book titled *How to Make Money with Social Media*, and we just said that not every campaign is supposed to generate revenue.

What do we mean by that?

Some very successful social media campaigns aren't designed to generate sales as much as they're designed to generate satisfied customers. Dan Gingiss, the Director of Digital Customer Experience and Social

Media for Discover Card, has a team of social media experts who monitor and review tweets and Facebook posts from customers. Discover is in a highly regulated industry, which makes responding to account-specific inquiries a challenge. But Discover has found ways to monitor the conversations and to take care of the customer's concerns either via a Twitter direct message or in a secure online chat environment.

The response has been very positive, with customers responding with praise for Discover's use of social media to handle customer service issues.

The idea behind this initiative is that Discover wanted to be able to answer customer questions in the channels in which the customer initiated the request. They also found that by participating in the online conversations in a personalized and genuine way, they were able to a) quickly solve the customer's problems, b) demonstrate their superior customer service in a public ways, and c) minimize the negative commentary from disgruntled cardholders, who often end up posting positive commentary after being serviced.

In this particular case, Discover is using social media as a customer service tool. Although it's difficult to assign a dollar amount to the value of a social customer service campaign, it's not impossible. For starters, you can track how much it costs to manage a customer complaint using traditional media and compare it to the cost of managing it via social media.

In the old days, customer service complaints were handled almost exclusively via an 800 number. That meant manning an entire bank of phones with operators who could only handle one customer complaint at a time. If the operators got busy, customers were put on hold. When an angry customer gets put on hold, they grow increasingly frustrated. By the time the operator gets to the now-frustrated customer, the operator has to spend time easing them back into a civil and productive conversation. It was an expensive way to manage customer service.

By comparing the cost of traditional customer service to the cost of social media customer service, companies such as Discover can make a calculation of whether or not they have improved efficiencies by using social media customer service. If the cost of having a traditional customer service department is, say, $1 million per year, but the cost of having a blended traditional and social customer service department is $900,000, then their social media efforts "made" the company $100,000.

Of course, that's a simplified view of the costs associated with a customer service department, but it highlights a larger issue—not all social media campaigns are designed to *make* money; some are designed to *save* money.

TOOLS, TIPS, AND TECHNIQUES

HootSuite and TweetDeck are two well-known but basic social media management tools. When you're ready to move up a notch, consider SproutSocial, Oktopost, or Rignite. Or, if you want to move into the world of social customer relationship management (CRM), take a look at Insightly, Nimble, Batchwork, or Oracle Social. These platforms add CRM tools to the equation, giving you the ability to better manage your interactions with prospects and customers.

The Dell Outlet campaign was designed to drive prospects to an e-commerce page, and the Discover campaign was designed as a customer service tool, but what if your campaign is designed for neither? What if your campaign is simply designed to keep customers engaged with your products or services? For example, what if you don't have an e-commerce page or a customer service department? How can you calculate the value of your social media campaign then?

That calculation isn't as difficult as you might imagine. One way to do it is to analyze social media's impact on your churn rate. If you're like most companies, you lose a certain number of customers or clients each year. That churn has a real impact on your business. If you're a $100 million corporation and 10 percent of your business leaves every year, that's $10 million in lost revenue you have to replace each year just to stay even.

But let's say you launch a social media campaign and are able to engage prospects and customers at such a rate that you reduce churn from 10 percent each year to 9.5 percent each year. That may not sound like much, but that 0.5 percent saves your company $500,000 in lost revenue.

If the cost of running your social media campaign was $200,000, then you just "made" your company $300,000!

This example shows again that a social media campaign can provide value to a company in a number of different ways. Sometimes, as in the case of Dell Outlet, it can be tied directly to revenue. But other times, as in the case of Discover and the aforementioned example, the formula is a little more nuanced.

No matter what, if you're going to run a successful campaign, it's important that you use a system of metrics that can help you calculate whether or not the campaign is working. If you're not tracking your results and tying them to revenue, then you're not optimizing social media for everything that it can be.

Okay, let's talk about what you can do with the information we just discussed. After all, learning new information is just half the battle. The other half is to apply the information so that it has an impact on your business.

Here are some things we'd like you to do as we wrap up this chapter:

- *Reframe your thinking.* Many people think about social media from a tactical basis. In other words, they think about Facebook pages and Twitter handles and Google+ profiles before they think about goals and objectives. If that includes you, we're going to ask you to change your perspective. Begin by identifying your goals and objectives for your campaign. Is it to drive leads? Is it to reduce churn? Or perhaps it's simply to create brand preference. In the long run, if you want to make money with social media, you have to start with the end in mind.

- *Start using social media management tools.* One of the biggest complaints people have about social media is that it takes so much effort to get real traction. Setting up a campaign isn't all that difficult, but getting people engaged and active on your sites takes a lot of time and effort. One of the ways around this is to move beyond social media *execution* and move into social media *management.* We'll cover social media management tools in the upcoming chapters, but if you want to jump online and get familiar with them right now, check out SproutSocial,

Rignite, Oktopost, HootSuite, Socialbakers, and Webfluenz, all of which are top-ranked social media management tools. When you're ready to go beyond social media management and move into social CRM, be sure to investigate Insightly, Nimble, and Batchwork.

- *Formalize your metrics.* The odds are pretty good that you're tracking some form of data around your social media campaigns, which is fine. But if you're using a back-of-the-envelope system to track your data, it's probably not doing you any good. Instead, start tracking your results using the dashboards available with some of the social media management tools mentioned in the previous bullet point. Alternatively, you can track your results on a Google spreadsheet that can be viewed (and edited) by other members of your team. It's surprising how things improve once they're tracked consistently and once people are held accountable for results.

- *Narrow your focus.* Many businesses jump into social media and spread themselves over a wide variety of platforms too quickly, which reduces their ability to run effective campaigns. If you believe you've spread yourself across too many platforms, it might be a good idea to scale back focus to only a handful of platforms. Once those platforms are running effectively, you can always scale back up. Remember, it's better to do a great job on three platforms than it is to do a mediocre job on 10.

Before we move on to the next chapter, let's take a look at the key concepts and action steps we've covered in this chapter:

- **Key concept**—Dell was one of the first companies to figure out how to use a social media platform to drive incremental revenue to their business.

- **Action step**—Explore ways that you can use the Dell Outlet model for your business. That may require an e-commerce landing page, which many businesses don't have. Even so, become familiar with their model because it's the foundation for much of what we'll be discussing in upcoming chapters.

- **Key concept**—Not all social media campaigns are designed to *make* money. Some are designed to *save* money.

- **Action step**—Are you using social media as a customer service tool? Perhaps you're using social media as a way to reduce churn. No matter how you're using social media, you should be making calculations about how it's impacting the bottom line on your business.

- **Key concept**—Reframe your thinking about social media.

- **Action step**—If your thought process around social media begins with tactics (Twitter, Facebook, Google+, and so on), do a flip-flop and start thinking about goals and objectives first. From there, you can move on to your strategy to help you accomplish your goals and objectives. Once you've worked through all of those, you're ready to move on to the tactical side of the equation.

Endnotes

1. http://marketingland.com/fortune-500-companys-social-media-use-on-the-rise-52726

2. http://www.emarketer.com/Article/Marketers-Still-Cant-Tie-Social-Bottom-Line/1009340

3. http://www.webinknow.com/2010/01/roi-rant.html

4. http://mashable.com/2009/06/11/delloutlet-two-million/

5. http://mashable.com/2009/12/08/dell-twitter-sales/

2

The Evolution of Marketing

The owners of the new Red's Porch,[1] located in a refurbished fire station in a trendy part of town, had a brilliant idea. They would use the viral power of social media to grow visibility and awareness of their new restaurant.

Their idea was simple, elegant, and oh-so-viral. They would send tweets that they'd provide a free drink extravaganza at their restaurant if they could get just 100 Twitter followers by the following Monday.

Free drinks. Open bar. No charge.

In the world of marketing, there are two sure-fire promotions. The first is to give away free money. The second is to give away free alcohol, which is exactly what the members of Red's Porch intended to do.

The promotion was so bold and so viral that the biggest concern was not whether it would work, but whether it would overheat the fledgling restaurant. After all, the mainstream media had written stories outlining the success of social media programs such as the one Red's was about to conduct.

Perhaps the best known of these success stories was the one about Dell Outlet, discussed in Chapter 1, "In the Beginning." The Twitter page was so successful that it garnered more than 1.5 million followers and generated more than $6.5 million in incremental revenue for Dell.

Given Dell's success, it wasn't surprising that the owners of Red's Porch worried that giving away free alcohol would overheat the restaurant. The fastest way to kill a good restaurant and bar is to drive too many people to a location, which leads to an overworked wait staff and customers who are frustrated by long lines and a backed-up kitchen.

The owners were a little anxious when they sent their first tweet:

> *Help us grow our Twitter list. If we get 100 followers by Monday, we will invite all to a free drinks party. OPEN BAR!!!*

They followed their initial tweet with several more tweets, all promoting one of the most bullet-proof promotions in the history of marketing— free alcohol. During the promotion, the owners checked in periodically to find out how many new followers they had generated.

Did they generate 1,000 new followers? 5,000 new followers? Perhaps 10,000?

Nope. They generated 23 new followers. Not 23 *hundred* or 23 *thousand*. Just 23.

What happened?

For starters, they didn't have something that we call **social media magnetism**.

With social media magnetism, your brand is so powerful that people are attracted to it the way metal is attracted to a magnet. Your brand has so much innate appeal that people go out of their way to be affiliated and associated with your company because it gives them a sense of style, cache, and panache.

Brands such as Nike, Coca-Cola, and Harley-Davidson have tons of social media magnetism, which is why you see people wearing Nike sweatshirts or putting Harley-Davidson logos on the rear window of their cars. (Think about it: When was the last time you saw a sweatshirt with a Joe's Plumbing or Nanci's Florist logo on it?)

The good news about social media magnetism is that, if you have it, you can grow your social media program organically. People actually *want* to be affiliated with brands that have social media magnetism. They want to have your logo on their car. They want to wear a sweatshirt with your logo on it. And they want to be a fan on your Facebook page.

To be a social media magnet, you usually have to spend millions of dollars and put in hundreds of thousands of man-hours. Nike, Coca-Cola, and Harley-Davidson didn't just happen. They were part of a concerted effort to build brands that had social media magnetism. And building those brands took decades, not days.

The second challenge our friends at Red's Porch had was that they were under the impression that creating a promotion was the first step in a social media campaign.

But it's not the first step—it's actually the *second* step. The first step is to use traditional media or word-of-mouth advertising to drive awareness and traffic to your Twitter, Facebook, YouTube, LinkedIn, or Pinterest page.

THE BIG IDEA

Most brands don't have social media magnetism, but that's okay—there are things you can do to address that.

Sure, if you have social media magnetism, you can easily skip the first step and jump to the second step. But if you're like most of us, you'll have to use a lot of the traditional methods to drive awareness. Those methods might include print, radio, and TV (if you're a large, well-funded brand), or they might include e-mail, public relations, and word-of-mouth (if you're a small, underfunded brand).

All this leads us to one of our key points: *You can waste a lot of time and money in social media if you don't map out a step-by-step strategy that points you toward your goals.*

That's why we wrote this book—to help people like you navigate through the world of social media and to help them map out an approach that will give them the results they're looking for.

Given all that, let's start with a fundamental premise—businesses don't develop social media campaigns because they want to be *social.* Instead, they develop social media campaigns because they want to *grow their sales and revenues.* More specifically, they want to do any combination of these three things:

- Acquire new customers.
- Get existing customers to come back again.
- Get customers to spend more at each purchase.

It's important to understand these three objectives because so many people get wrapped up in the minutia of social media that they lose track of the overall objectives of virtually any campaign.

To illustrate the importance of setting goals and establishing objectives, let's take a quick look at some of the foundations of marketing that have happened over the past 150 years. By taking a look back at where marketing has been, we'll have an even better sense of how to move forward in the future.

Where Marketing Has Been

The first marketing communications firms (then known as advertising agents) started in the 1860s and 1870s. At that time, companies such as N. W. Ayer and J. Walter Thompson wrote the ads and then charged companies a 15 percent commission for publishing them in newspapers and magazines.

In the 1930s and 1940s, the great advertising agencies such as Leo Burnett and Ogilvy & Mather were born. They did such a magnificent job at selling products to consumers that, by the 1950s and 1960s, corporations were clamoring to get the top agencies on Madison Avenue to work on their accounts. CEOs of the world's largest corporations took CEOs of advertising agencies out to dinner to discuss business, profits, and this mysterious new thing called *marketing*.

The agencies had something that the corporations couldn't get their hands on—*creative people.* These were the (mostly) men portrayed on television as martini-drinking, skirt-chasing prima donnas whose magic touch on an ad could make the difference between a profitable quarter and an unprofitable one.

Ahhh, if it were still only that simple.

By the 1980s, the power began to shift away from Madison Avenue to the corporations themselves. Corporations seemed to believe that their success revolved not around the creative, but around *strategy.* They thought that the most important part of a marketing campaign wasn't the headline or the visual; it was the *strategy* behind the headline or the visual.

The people who could think up the best strategies came from schools such as Stanford, Harvard, and Wharton. So the corporations started hiring MBAs, and the power shifted away from Madison Avenue to the corporate side of the equation.

This was all fine and dandy—if you were on the corporate side. However, the ad agencies weren't too happy about the shift in power. Even so, they accepted the changes and began establishing expertise in other areas, which made them just as important to the overall success of their clients' businesses.

Fast-forward to the 1990s, when data and information became the king and queen of marketing. Suddenly, the center of power wasn't in the advertising agencies. Nor was it with the brand managers on the corporate level. It shifted to retailers (such as Walmart, Home Depot, and Office Depot), who, with their highly sophisticated logistics and data management programs, were able to slice and dice information to such a degree that they could tweak distribution not only on a city-by-city level, but also on a store-by-store level.

That power shift—from the ad agency, to the corporation, to the retailer—all happened during the last half of the twentieth century. For decades, the advertising gurus on Madison Avenue were in charge of the brand. Then the MBAs took over. And for a while, the retailers were in charge.

But today, a quantum shift has occurred in who controls the conversation about the brand. It's no longer solely the agency, the corporation, or the retailer. *It's the customer.* The customer is in charge of your brand as much as you are, and what they think and say about it can spread around the globe at the speed of light (see Figure 2.1).

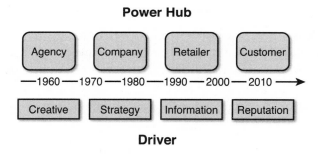

Source: Dr. Reshma Shah, Emory University

Figure 2.1 The power brokers in marketing have evolved during the past 50 years.

In 1965, a brand such as Coca-Cola or Pepsi could communicate with 85 percent of the viewing TV audience by running three prime-time commercials. That's right, any brand that could run just three commercials in prime time could connect with the vast majority of people who were watching TV.

But by 2014, the same brands had to run more than 130 commercials to achieve the same results. Why? Because of the fragmentation of the viewing audience across dozens (or hundreds) of cable channels.

Then, with the wide adoption of broadband Internet, platforms such as YouTube, Facebook, LinkedIn, Twitter, Google+, and Pinterest took center stage. When content distribution shifted to those platforms, the consumer started having as much control over the brand as the agency, the corporation, or the retailer.

Social Media Comes of Age

Yes, the consumer has taken control of your brand. For evidence of this, just ask United Airlines. In a well-known incident that happened several years ago, more than 13 million people watched a YouTube video titled "United Breaks Guitars," written by a musician named Dave Carroll after the airline allegedly refused to repair his guitar that was broken on a United flight. According to one source, the company's stock price dropped nearly 10 percent the week after the video went viral.

Or ask Epicurious.com, the website for food lovers around the globe. When two terrorists set off bombs at the Boston Marathon, Epicurious Tweeted, "Boston, our hearts are with you. Here's a bowl of breakfast energy we could all use to start the day...." The victims of the Boston Marathon attack, along with the rest of the world, were not amused.

Or what about Pepsi? A division of the cola giant released a set of Facebook ads featuring a voodoo doll of Portuguese football (or soccer) player Cristiano Ronaldo tied to train tracks, covered in pins. The ads didn't go over very well. So much so that a Portuguese anti-Pepsi Facebook group gained over 100,000 followers in a single day. It wasn't long before Pepsi removed the ads and apologized for running them in the first place.

The bottom line is this: If you're a brand manager, a chief marketing officer, or anybody who has an interest in the success of your marketing program (which should be 100 percent of the people working at your company), you should be aware that you no longer own your company's brand. The customer does. And that's both an opportunity and a threat.

THE BIG IDEA

Consumers have as much control over your brand's perception as you do. By remaining genuine and transparent, and by nurturing your relationship with them, you can create brand advocates who will do much of the selling for you.

We've covered several important concepts in this chapter, so let's review them and take a look at some of the action steps around them:

- **Key concept**—A social media magnet is a brand that people naturally gravitate to. The odds are your brand is not a social media magnet, but fear not—we can fix that.

- **Action step**—Deepen your understanding of your customers' emotional hot buttons. Explore ways to tap into what it is that motivates them to buy your product or service. Many people buy products for emotional reasons. By understanding your customers' hot buttons and exploring them, you can create a deeper, more meaningful relationship via your social media campaigns.

- **Key concept**—Successful social media campaigns are designed to do three things: 1) acquire new customers, 2) get existing customers to buy again, and 3) get customers to spend more at each purchase.

- **Action step**—Don't lose sight of those three goals as you build your social media campaign. It's very common for social media managers to shift their attention from important goals (such as the three mentioned here) to less important goals such as deadlines, content generation, and execution. Remember, all roads in social media should lead to ROI, and ROI only happens when you focus on the three goals mentioned here.

- **Key concept**—The center of power for your brand is no longer the agency, the corporation, or the retailer. It's the consumer.

> - **Action step**—Honor the consumer in everything you do. Be transparent. Learn from the mistakes other corporations have made when they've attempted to mask or hide corporate secrets or hot topics. It's better to come clean and be genuine. By doing so, you'll give consumers what they need to become advocates for your brand.

Endnotes

1. The Red's Porch case study is based on a real restaurant and actual events. We've changed the name to protect the innocent.

3

How to Think Strategically about Social Media

One of the biggest challenges with social media is that most people run their campaigns in reverse order.

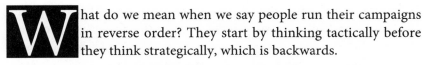hat do we mean when we say people run their campaigns in reverse order? They start by thinking tactically before they think strategically, which is backwards.

A typical approach is to kick things off by saying, "We need a Facebook page. And a Twitter profile. And a Pinterest board!" But that's the wrong way to go about it. The right way is to say, "We need a goal. And an objective. And a strategy." If you start your campaigns by focusing on goals and objectives first, then you can work your way through to strategies, tactics, and executional approaches after that. The result is that you'll have a sense of where you're going before you get started.

Think of it this way—if you wanted to drive from Atlanta to Austin, you'd start by establishing your goal (to get to Austin), then think through your objective (to get there within five days without running out of gas), and then settle in on a strategy that'll help you achieve your goal and objective (to break the trip into five bite-sized chunks with stops every three hours to refuel and use the rest area).

Does that make sense?

We'll cover the specifics about goals, objectives, strategies, and tactics in Chapter 18, "Establishing Your Major Objectives and Key Strategies," but for now, let's shift gears a little bit and explore how to think strategically about your business, your customers, and, ultimately, your next social media campaign.

A great place to start this exercise is by examining the motivations that drive your customers to buy your products or services in the first place. On the surface, you probably believe that your customers are buying the features of your products or services. So, for example, if you're Maid Brigade, a national home cleaning service, you'd say that your customers are buying a clean house. After all, when someone calls Maid Brigade, that customer doesn't ask them to mow their lawn—they ask them to clean their house.

But is that really what they're asking for?

Oh, sure, a clean house is an essential element of what Maid Brigade is selling, but there are plenty of businesses that clean houses. So the question really becomes, "In addition to a clean house, what is it that a Maid Brigade customer is *really* buying?"

For starters, they're buying a brand they trust. For some companies (such as Coca-Cola and Apple), the value of the brand is one of their most important assets. For perspective on the value of a brand, consider this—in your neighborhood, there are probably several local restaurants that sell pizza. And many of those restaurants sell better pizza than Domino's. But Domino's almost certainly *sells more pizzas per store than any of the restaurants in your neighborhood.*

Why? Because Domino's has a national brand that people have grown to love and trust. And, when it comes right down to it, love and trust translates into big bucks—and more pizzas sold.

Now that we've talked about the value of a brand, let's jump back to the Maid Brigade case study. People don't hire Maid Brigade simply because they're a trustworthy national brand or because they do a good job cleaning houses. It goes much deeper than that. When you drill down into what prompts someone to buy their services, you start to uncover some of the *unspoken* reasons why people gravitate to their brand.

For example, Maid Brigade was the first national chain to go green with their cleaning materials. So, a certain percentage of people hire Maid Brigade because they like the *green* aspect of their services. For most people, "green cleaning" isn't the very first thing they're looking for when they do research on home cleaning services, but it's certainly a key differentiator for their brand.

But we're still just scratching the surface—you can go much deeper. For example, what is it that people really get when they get a clean house? People get more than just a clean house—they also get *time*. In other words, they free up several hours a week that they would otherwise spend cleaning.

What do they get in those several hours? Initially, you might say they get time to play more tennis, time with the grandchildren, or time to work with a charity. All of those answers are correct, but when you examine it further, you realize that customers are actually getting the opportunity to have more fulfilling lives, to have deeper relationships, and to get to know themselves better.

See how that works? What people are actually buying in a product or service goes much deeper than you might imagine.

If you were to write down a list of the features and benefits of using Maid Brigade, you would likely just scratch the surface. But by getting inside the mind of the customer and thinking about what truly motivates them, you come up with emotional hot buttons that resonate with their prospects and customers.

Again, that's not to say that you shouldn't *lead* with "green clean" or "spotless counters" or "freshly vacuumed rug." Those aspects of the Maid Brigade brand are all important, but when you overlay those benefits with the deeper, more meaningful emotional hot buttons, you connect with your prospects and customers on a more lasting basis.

TOOLS, TIPS, AND TECHNIQUES

No matter what business you're in, one of your primary goals is to drive traffic to your website. Google Analytics measures that traffic, but did you know that there are plenty of good alternatives? KISSmetrics, Fox-Metrics, and Adobe Analytics are all designed to give you a fresh and innovative look at the data around your website.

Here's an Exercise We'd Like You to Do

Grab a sheet of paper and write down a list of all the reasons someone buys a cup of coffee from Starbucks. We'd like you to think about *what motivates someone to buy a cup of Starbucks coffee.*

First on your list, of course, is that customers simply want a cup of coffee. That's reason enough. But what else are they buying? Aren't they also buying the "cool" factor at Starbucks? Aren't they buying the fact that Starbucks is often populated with young, trend-setting professionals? And aren't they buying the way the Starbucks environment makes them feel?

What else? You can go even deeper. Some people are buying the friendly smile from the barista. Others are buying the trendy music playing in the background. And still others are buying the cushy sofas that are perfect for people working on laptops.

Going deeper still, you realize that some people are there *because they feel lonely.* And, interestingly, some people are there because they *want to be alone.*

Others are there because it helps them think...or daydream...or clear their minds.

And, of course, eventually we come full circle and realize that some people are at Starbucks simply because they want a darn good cup of coffee.

Our point, whether you're talking about Maid Brigade or Starbucks or any other company, is that the foundation for any successful social media campaign is to *explore the motivations that are driving your customers to buy your products or services in the first place.* The odds are pretty good that they're buying much more than just the features and benefits—they're buying the *hidden value* of your products and services as well.

Your customers are buying more than just your products or services. They're also buying something that fills a deep emotional need that isn't always obvious. By understanding your customer's emotional motivations, you're laying the foundation for a much more effective social media campaign.

Wrapping Your Mind around Social Media

Now that we've talked about how to gain a deep understanding of your prospects and customers, let's lay the foundation for how to *think* about social media. The easiest way to do that is to draw comparisons to other things you might be familiar with, so let's start with social media in general.

What is social media? You can find dozens of answers on the Internet, some helpful and some flat wrong. But for our purposes, social media is made up of digital tools that prompt a dialogue between your customers and your business.

Unfortunately, many businesses use social media for one-way monologues instead of two-way dialogues. This brings us to an important point:

Social media is more like a telephone than it is a megaphone.

Businesses that use social media as a megaphone are using it incorrectly. You know the kind of businesses we're talking about. They can't stop talking about themselves and what makes their products or services special. But have you ever been on a date with someone who can't stop talking about how wonderful he or she is? Have you ever been out with someone who constantly bragged and never once asked you about your interests?

We're guessing here, but we imagine that if you went on a date with someone like that, it was probably the last date you had with him or her.

So back to our analogy—when you're running your next social media campaign, think of the platforms you're using as tools that are more like telephones than they are megaphones.

Key Social Media Platforms

Now let's take that analogy a step further. If using social media is similar to using a telephone, then what is Facebook like? Or LinkedIn? Or Twitter?

We developed some analogies to help frame your thinking:

- *Facebook is like a pub.* It's a casual place where you can go to talk about what you did over the weekend, tell a joke, or tell people what you did at your high school reunion.

- *Google+ is like a country club.* Despite the fact that Google+ is one of the fastest-growing social media networks on the planet and has a wide-ranging user base, it still has an exclusive feel to it because it remains clean, uncluttered, and (for the moment) free from advertising.

- *LinkedIn is like a trade show.* You wouldn't tell people at a trade show what you did in Vegas last weekend, would you? Okay, maybe *you* would, but the average businessperson wouldn't. Limit LinkedIn to your professional side. Talk about business. Talk about interesting articles in the *Harvard Business Review*. And use plenty of phrases such as "value chain" and "business model" in your profile. That should do the trick.

- *Twitter is like a cocktail party.* Cocktail parties are great places to mingle, share information, and make new friends—just like millions of people do every day on Twitter. It may be a bit of a challenge to pack a lot of information into 140 characters, but if you can master that aspect of Twitter, you'll be able to use it quite effectively for business.

- *Pinterest is like a bulletin board.* The whole idea behind Pinterest is that it's a place for people to share thoughts, ideas, photographs, favorite quotes, and other pieces of information on a series of digital bulletin boards that can be seen and shared by others. Most businesses use Pinterest as a branding tool to deepen their relationship with prospects and customers, but others are using it (quite effectively) to provide information about special promotions or product offerings.

- *YouTube is like Times Square on New Year's Eve.* Times Square on New Year's Eve is packed with people clamoring for attention, which illustrates the problem. Just as it's hard to stand out in Times Square, it's hard to stand out on YouTube. Too much competition exists. So if you want to use YouTube to make money, you need to build awareness for your YouTube channel first.

DID YOU KNOW?

The monthly viewership on YouTube is more than one billion people, which is the equivalent of roughly ten Super Bowl audiences. And if YouTube were a country, it would be the third largest country in the world.[1]

Other Social Media Platforms You Should Know About

One of the more common mistakes people make when thinking about social media is to think that social media is about only Facebook, Google+, LinkedIn, Twitter, YouTube, and Pinterest. In reality, social media is about much more.

For our purposes, we're including the following categories on our list of tools you can use to grow your sales and revenues using social media:

- **Blogs and digital magazines**—These are quickly becoming many people's primary source of news and information.

- **Bookmarks and tags**—Similar to digital yellow stickies that let other members of the online community know that you like an article or a web page.

- **E-mail newsletters**—Digital flyers that let people know about your products or services.

- **Widgets**—Online gadgets that help you crunch numbers, check the weather, or find out how much money you made (or lost) in the stock market.

- **Content aggregation sites**—Sites that effectively cut out articles from other online newspapers and repost them in one central location.

- **Wikis**—Sites that enable large groups of people to contribute and edit content.

- **Voting**—Provides people the opportunity to express their opinion on a product or service.

- **Crowdsourcing**—Uses the talents of many people in different parts of the globe to contribute to something (such as the development of an open-source software program).

- **Discussion boards and forums**—Places where people can digitally thumbtack their thoughts, comments, or suggestions on a digital corkboard hosted on your website.

- **Backchannel sites**—Places where people at trade shows and conventions can comment on the event or the speaker on stage.

- **Tweetups**—Meetings or casual get-togethers that are organized via Twitter. ("Meet us as Bob's Tavern at 6:00 pm. We're getting together to discuss the top social media campaigns from this year.")

- **Photo-sharing sites**—Digital photo albums on sites such as Flickr, Instagram, and Snapfish where people can upload their favorite photos.

- **Podcasting**—A way for small and large organizations to broadcast their thoughts, comments, or perspectives on a wide variety of topics.

- **Presentation-sharing sites**—Places where you can upload your latest and greatest PowerPoints.

- **Virtual worlds**—Places where (young) people go to create second lives.

- **Ratings and reviews**—Enable people to rate your product or service and write reviews. (Believe it or not, negative reviews can actually help your brand because they give you instant customer feedback.)

Social Media Models Used by the Fortune 500

Whether you work as a sole proprietor or at a Fortune 500 company, it's a good idea to know how others are using social media so you can incorporate those models into your own campaigns.

With that in mind, here are five social media models used by the Fortune 500:

- **Branding**—Some companies use social media strictly as a branding tool. Typically, this means running a YouTube campaign that (hopefully) gets a lot of buzz around the water cooler. In our opinion, using social media only as a branding tool is a twentieth-century mindset. If you really want to supercharge your social media campaigns, you'll incorporate one or all of the next four highly measurable approaches.

- **E-commerce**—If you can sell your product or service online, then you'll want to drive people to a landing page on your website where they can buy your goods. How can you accomplish this? Just do what many e-commerce companies do and post special promotions available only to the people who follow them on social media. The promotional links are easily tracked so they can see how many people went to the landing page and how many converted from a prospect to a customer.

- **Research**—Many companies are using social media as a tool to do research. Sometimes, this involves building a website to track the results. Starbucks has done this famously with their MyStarbucksIdea.com website. Other times, using social media as a research tool can be as simple as conducting a poll on LinkedIn, SurveyMonkey, or via e-mail.

- **Customer retention**—A good rule of thumb is that it costs three to five times as much to acquire a new customer than it does to keep an existing one. Given that, wouldn't it be smart to use social media as a tool to keep customers loyal and engaged? That's what Comcast and Southwest Airlines do—they communicate via Twitter, Facebook, and other social media platforms to help solve customer service issues.

- **Lead generation**—What do you do if you can't sell your product or service online? Then you'll want to do what many B2B companies do—that is, they use social media to drive prospects to a website where they can download a whitepaper, listen to a podcast, or watch a video. Once you've captured the prospect's contact information, you can re-market to them via e-mail, direct mail, or any number of other methods.

Let's review several key concepts and action steps from this chapter before we move on:

- **Key concept**—It's easy to wrap your mind around social media when you draw parallels between it and something you're already familiar with.

- **Action step**—Review the different parallels between platforms such as YouTube, Facebook, and Twitter and things you're already familiar with (such as a pub). Share those parallels with people in your office who might not be as familiar with social media as you are. That way, they can get comfortable with these new tools, too.

- **Key concept**—Social media is about more than just YouTube, Facebook, Twitter, Pinterest, and LinkedIn.

- **Action step**—Broaden your understanding of the various social media tools by visiting several blogs, forums, e-newsletters, and other platforms you might not have visited.

- **Key concept**—There are five different social media models used by the Fortune 500.

- **Action step**—Use one or more of these models for your own social media campaign. Better still, evolve one of these into a brand-new approach that's even better than these originals.

Endnote

1. http://youtube-global.blogspot.com/2013/03/onebillionstrong.html

4

How to Speak Social Media

You're interested in learning how to use social media to grow your sales and revenue. That's good. But before we dive into the specifics of making money with social media, we need to talk about the language of social media. After all, the starting point of any good conversation is language, right?

One of the big issues surrounding the language of social media is whether it's singular or plural. The word *media* is plural, but we're not big fans of saying, "Social media *are* important marketing tools," when most people are saying, "Social media *is* an important marketing tool."

We're aware that we're breaking all sorts of rules by doing that, but we're reasonably sure our use of social media in the singular won't lead to the downfall of Western civilization. Our goal in the conversation we're having with you is to talk with you in plain, honest language that's as clear and easy to understand as possible.

Make sense?

Getting Social Media Vocabulary Straight

We should discuss a few other terms before we continue, such as the differences in a social medium, a platform, and a channel:

- **Social medium**—Any single, broad category of tool that you use to run a social media campaign. A blog, a forum, and a user-generated video site are all examples of a social medium.

- **Platform**—The software or technology you use within a social medium. For example, WordPress is a platform used for blogging, and YouTube is a platform used for online video.

- **Channel**—The specific, individual connection between you and your customer. Examples of social media channels include your specific blog, Twitter account, and Facebook profile.

We need to explain one thing that might have been on your mind. Many people have described social media as a silver bullet for your business. They've written blog posts, posted YouTube videos, and even written books talking about how social media is "transformative" and "the next big thing." (Yes, we see the irony in this.)

The result is that social media can sometimes be viewed as a panacea to all your marketing and business problems.

Social media isn't a cure for everything that ails your business. And it's not a silver bullet that you can turn on to solve all your problems. But it is a viable, long-lasting marketing tool that, when used properly, can help you grow revenues, increase customer loyalty, and build awareness. And that's not such a bad thing, right?

The Social Media Life Cycle

Social media isn't the first new technology to be overhyped. Think back a few years ago when web logs, now known as *blogs*, gained traction. Corporations, nonprofit groups, and individuals all jumped onto the blogging bandwagon.

The more these entities adopted blogging as a viable communications tool, the more blogs were positioned as a silver bullet that would easily solve just about any marketing problem. For a while, it seemed as though every CEO at a Fortune 500 company had a blog.

But then a funny thing happened. People realized that blogs weren't going to solve all their problems, so they grew disenchanted. Suddenly, people viewed blogs as a waste of time. People decided they didn't have time for blogs, especially blogs that nobody read.

But blogs didn't die. They just evolved into something better and more useful. Instead of using blogs as press release distribution tools, CEOs (and other members of corporations) began using individual blogs as channels to have *conversations* with their prospects and customers. When the conversations happened, people began to recognize how to best use a blog.

Companies now realize that their blogs are channels that can create a link between a customer or prospect and a business. And when they build that link, they're creating loyalty for their brand and their product or service.

The same thing has happened with social media. At first, it was over-hyped and people viewed it as a quick-and-easy way to grow their sales and revenues. Then, some people grew disenchanted and said it was a waste of their efforts. But now, people have figured out how to use it effectively and how to generate a positive ROI for their efforts.

TOOLS, TIPS, AND TECHNIQUES

Want to supercharge your Facebook page? WooBox and Agorapulse offer some great tools for Facebook promotions. You can also use Like-alyzer to analyze and monitor your pages.

Bringing Your Social Media Campaign to Life

The model illustrated in Figure 4.1 isn't the only social media business model, but it's the model that companies such as Dell and Papa John's Pizza have used to build their social media programs. Essentially, customer prospects are driven to social media channels that the parent company sponsors or manages. In Dell's case, the company uses Twitter.com/DellOutlet as a way to promote special offers to the millions of people who follow them on that Twitter page. When a special offer is posted on the DellOutlet page, it drives customer prospects to a landing page on the company's website that has been specifically set up to match the offer on the DellOutlet page. If the offer is appealing enough, a small percentage of Dell prospects will convert to Dell customers. With that data and information now captured in their system, Dell can remarket to those members of the Dell social media community who landed on the Dell site via Twitter.

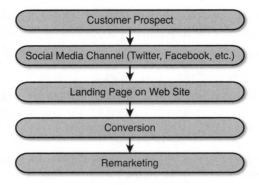

Figure 4.1 You can measure social media on a return on investment (ROI) basis, particularly if you use business models such as this one.

To drive prospects to the social media channel, Dell (or any other corporation) can use different types of traditional and nontraditional media. The company could use direct mail, TV, radio, or outdoor advertising to make people aware of the social media community it has created. Or, more likely, Dell could use blogs, forums, and online video to generate traffic. And if a company is really sophisticated, it uses contextual advertising or behavior targeting to drive traffic to its social media site.

A **contextual ad** is a paid search or online display ad placed near similar content on a blog, an app, or online article. If you own a hunting lodge in Montana and you want to attract customers to your lodge, it would make sense to place a display ad near an article or blog post that's about rifles, shotguns, hunting, or other outdoor activities, right? By running ads that are contextually sensitive, you increase the click-through rate. And when you increase the click-through rate, you increase your profits.

Ahhh, profits. Nice!

What about behavioral targeting? What's that all about? **Behavioral targeting** is similar to contextual ads, but with a few important differences. Behaviorally targeted ads follow groups of people around the Internet. For example, tens of thousand of people each day type "cameras" or "camera gear" into Google, Yahoo!, or Bing. A certain percentage of those people click through to websites that contain information about cameras that'll help them make decisions about their next camera purchase. But most people don't finalize their decisions about buying a camera in just a few clicks. Typically, they surf the Web on several different occasions, continuing to gather information before they spend $900 on a new camera.

Wouldn't it be cool if, as those people surfed the Web, they saw an ad for your brand of camera? Wouldn't the click-through rate be higher if ads for your camera gear followed people around the Internet as they surfed for more information about cameras?

That's behavioral targeting, and it's a great way to make the shopping and purchase experience even more relevant.

Now, before you get all up-in-arms about privacy issues, remember that advertisers aren't following *you* around—they're following *statistical data* around. Nobody is snooping around your computer. They're just serving up ads to websites that thousands of people like you happen to be reading on a topic of interest that you share.

DID YOU KNOW?

Privacy advocates have raised some questions about behavioral targeting, but behavioral targeting uses the same techniques that the direct mail industry has been using for decades. The direct mail industry uses statistical data about large groups of people to send targeted messages to interested buyers. Behavioral targeting uses the same techniques.

So how does this relate to the social media model we outlined previously? It's an example of how savvy businesses can use tools such as contextual ads and behavioral targeting to drive people to social media sites. Once they're at the social media sites, businesses can ultimately drive them through to landing pages where they can buy products or services.

Some people might ask, "Why wouldn't I use contextual ads or behavioral targeting to drive people *directly* to my landing page? Why would I send them to my social media sites first?"

That's definitely one approach. Driving people directly to your landing page is a quick, easy way to introduce people to your products or services. But what happens when you start losing efficiencies on that model? What happens when people aren't clicking through on those ads as frequently as they used to?

When that happens, you add the next component, which is to use every form of media that you can (both traditional and nontraditional) to drive people to your social media channels. It's an additional way to add volume to your overall marketing campaign. Better still, it's an additional way to build a relationship with your customers and prospects.

Keeping Customers for Life

The concept of a relationship is worth pausing and thinking about for a second. Remember when we said that the whole idea behind a social media campaign is to have a two-way conversation with your customers and prospects? When you have a two-way conversation with customers and prospects, you're doing more than just having a conversation. You're building a *relationship*, too. Relationships happen over time, and they often happen *before your customer is ready to buy*.

Why is this so important? Because not all your customers are ready to buy at the same time. One consumer behavior model that highlights this is the Awareness, Interest, Desire, and Action (AIDA) model. This model has been used since the 1960s to highlight the process that consumers go through when they buy a product. If one person is in the awareness stage and another person is in the action stage, they have different buying mindsets. If you do things right, you'll send different pieces of communication to each of those consumers to address where they are on the AIDA decision-making process.

Let's look at a quick illustration of how to use the AIDA model when thinking about your social media campaign. If someone buys a car every five years, wouldn't it be a good idea to begin nurturing your relationship with that consumer in advance of the five-year mark? Absolutely.

The fact is, marketers frequently use consumer insights to improve the efficiencies of their campaigns. Auto manufacturers not only know what cars you bought previously, they also know your behaviors around your favorite ways to buy a car. So, if you typically buy a car every five years during the Spring Sale-a-Thon and always go for a $1,000 down lease, they'll start sending you targeted messages starting in January so that they have plenty of time to build awareness, generate interest, create desire, and, ultimately, encourage you to take action.

The advent of digital marketing and the introduction of Big Data (massive amounts of data that can be used to analyze consumer behavior) have made all sorts of amazing things possible for marketers. The result is that marketers are finding better and better ways to optimize their campaigns. And optimized campaigns result in more money toward the bottom line, which is always nice.

Let's recap a few of the key concepts we've covered and talk about action steps for those concepts:

- **Key concept**—A social medium is the category of tool a company is using to run a campaign (for example, blogs). A platform is the technology used within a social medium (for example, Facebook). And a channel is the specific, individual connection between the company and the customer (for example, a Facebook page).

- **Action step**—Learn these terms so that everyone within your company is using the same language to discuss your social media campaign.

- **Key concept**—Many different corporations are using several social media models. The most common model is customer/prospect → social media channel → landing page → conversion → remarketing.

- **Action step**—Set up your social media campaign so that it follows this basic model, which enables you to track results, adjust your campaign, and improve your ROI.

- **Key concept**—You can use traditional media and nontraditional media to drive traffic to your social media sites. The more traffic you drive to these sites, the more opportunity you have to build a long-term relationship with these prospects.

- **Action step**—Nurture your relationship with your prospects by providing them with useful tools and information that benefits them. Don't always sell, sell, sell. Sometimes a more nurturing, helpful approach builds deeper loyalty.

- **Key concept**—The Awareness, Interest, Desire, and Action (AIDA) model is a consumer behavior model that highlights where people are in the buying process.

- **Action step**—Customize your marketing campaigns so that they talk to prospects differently, depending on where they are in the buying cycle.

5

Laying the Groundwork for Success

The average tenure for a chief marketing officer at a midsize to large corporation is just 11 months. That's pretty scary.

Part of the problem is that most CMOs have difficulty figuring out how to measure their marketing campaigns. That's understandable—just a few years ago, the formula for marketing success was to develop a 30-second television spot and run the heck out of it.

Things have changed since then.

Back in the day, if you had a 30-second spot that made people laugh or cry, you were sitting pretty. And if that emotional connection actually resulted in *sales*, crazy things could happen for you, including promotions and raises.

Why was this? During the twentieth century, marketing was more about the *creative* than it was about the *media*. In other words, it was more important to have a fun and engaging commercial than it was to figure out where or when to run the commercial. If you were lucky and had a successful TV spot on your hands, you'd keep pumping more money into the campaign and watch sales rise. You'd continue with that approach until sales started to lag. Then you'd start everything all over again with a new campaign.

Figure 5.1 illustrates our point. The *y*-axis represents marketing expenditures, and the *x*-axis represents sales. The slope *(m)* represents the impact marketing has on sales. The steeper the slope, the greater the impact.

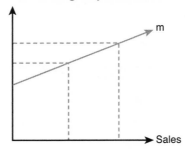

Marketing Expenditures

Figure 5.1 The slope (m) represents the impact marketing has on sales.

So, for example, if you were Geico and had another successful, funny commercial on your hands (that is, a commercial that had emotional appeal *and* made the cash register ring), you would continue adding to the marketing budget as long as the slope was in positive territory.

An example of a slightly more complex formula for all this is

$$a + bx_1 + cx_2 + dx_3 + ex_4 = y$$

where a = traditional media, b = social media, c = price, d = distribution, e = product mix, and y = profits. The variables signified by x_1, x_2, x_3, and x_4 all influence the campaign and will ultimately have an impact on the profits.

In the end, whether you're using complex formulas like this one, or simply calculating the success of your campaigns on a pad of paper, your goal is the same—to generate a positive ROI.

Measuring What Counts

Consider this interesting statistic: According to a survey by Mzinga and Babson Executive Education, only 16 percent of those polled said they currently measured the return on investment (ROI) for their social media programs (see Figure 5.2). More than four in ten respondents didn't even know whether the social tools they were using had ROI measurement capabilities.

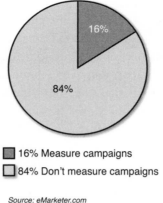

**Professionals Worldwide Who
Measure the ROI of Social Media**

16%

84%

■ 16% Measure campaigns
□ 84% Don't measure campaigns

Source: eMarketer.com

Figure 5.2 According to one survey, only 16 percent of marketers around the globe measure their social media campaigns on an ROI basis.

You don't have to be one of the 84 percent who don't measure the ROI of their social media campaigns. You can be one of the 16 percent who can track the results—if you follow the plan outlined in this book.

Not long ago, Rupal Mamtani, the founder and CEO of upscale furniture store Global Living, said, "I spend almost two to three hours a day personally on the social media marketing efforts for Global Living. I have to be the one involved. I can't outsource my Tweets. No one else has the perspective around this business the way I do. I represent the brand. Having said that, it's exhausting running the business 24/7 and managing to be the face of the brand."

When asked about the impact all her effort has had on her company's performance, she said, "After six months of being somewhat of a pioneer in the social media space in my industry, I am just now beginning to see results. People are beginning to engage more with me and with the company." She has not seen a direct impact on sales yet, but she sees more engagement, which could result in leads. *Leads*, she reiterates—not sales. For this CEO, social media is a supplement to traditional media, at best: "It won't replace newspaper advertising, a billboard, or even an event—at least, not in my business."

Clearly, Mamtani sees value in her social media involvement but still wonders when she'll see a return on the personal time she invests. Of course, the primary purpose of any kind of traditional marketing communication is to inform, persuade, or remind your customers about your product or service in an attempt to gain either a new sale or repeat sales. In the process, the hope is that your customers will become engaged with your organization or brand in a meaningful way that encourages them to keep coming back for more.

The good news for Mamtani is that she ultimately has her sights set on the only thing that really matters: social media's impact on sales. The fact that she's just beginning to see a link between the two is good news and, hopefully, is a sign of better things to come.

TOOLS, TIPS, AND TECHNIQUES

Want to monitor the mentions of your brand online? Be sure to set up Google Alerts. Or, for a more robust experience, check out Mention.com, which allows you to monitor, analyze, and collaborate with others.

Risks Associated with Social Media Campaigns

One multidivisional communications company we interviewed saw the benefits of engaging in social media but also identified several risks associated with it. The company currently has no formal organizational structure for managing the social media platforms and conversations across areas within the company, between the corporate office and the satellite locations, and between the company's buyers and sellers.

To ensure that conversations through social media marketing are meaningful, the company makes a large investment in people, technology, and processes. The company also believes that it will have to invest a great deal in research to understand just how social media impacts sales compared to other forms of marketing. With platforms and tools in social media evolving so rapidly, marketing heads are much more comfortable adopting a "wait and see" approach, to avoid making inefficient and ineffective investments in the social media space. And they're not alone.

Recent conversations with the chief marketing officer of another multibillion-dollar multidivisional company uncovered a similar sentiment. It's clear that this company understands the importance of adopting social media for its brands; however, the main concern is scalability. How can several thousand people connected though some common platform at a given point in time spark millions of consumers to take action?

CORPORATE SOCIAL MEDIA GUIDELINES

Many corporations have created employee guidelines for using social media on the job. Consider some essential guidelines:

- **Show respect**—Treat others with courtesy and respect.
- **Show responsibility**—Think before you communicate.
- **Demonstrate integrity**—Show sound moral character.
- **Be ethical**—Would your grandmother like what you're doing? If not, don't do it.
- **Add value**—Say something that moves the ball forward. Add to the conversation.

Fortunately, solutions to these challenges are starting to emerge. Corporations are developing social media guidelines for employees and are using enterprise social media management tools such as Oracle Social, Socialbakers, and Webfluenz to manage social media conversations around the globe.

This brings us to our final point, which deals with an organization's capability to achieve its desired brand positioning via social media. We would be very rich if we collected a dollar each time we heard a CMO confess to being unsure about investing in the resources required to adopt a social media strategy. So many of them hire interns from prestigious universities to help them "figure it out" and "determine the ROI" of such an investment—at least, that has been the norm in the most recent past. But hiring a few recent graduates to handle something as important as social media is a prescription for disaster, which is why we recommend assigning your social media program to a more seasoned employee or group of employees.

Social Media Isn't Free

The bottom line is that any effort requires investment. Sometimes this is an investment in people. Sometimes it's an investment in technology. Often it simply boils down to an investment in time.

When you're thinking about how you can use social media to connect with your customers and, ultimately, make money, ask yourself these key questions:

- Will the benefits of engaging in social media marketing outweigh the risks? Are there any risks if you do participate?

- Does your industry, product, or brand have a unique characteristic that may make social media more or less critical and relevant?

- Can you use social media marketing to influence key stakeholders in the intended manner?

- Do you know which platforms will resonate best with your stakeholders, and can you motivate them to participate?

- Does your organization have the necessary capabilities—including resources and processes—to achieve your desired brand positioning through social media?

- Do you have a way to integrate social media into your current marketing communications strategy?

- Do you have a set of metrics that will help you understand whether the return from social media was worth the investment?

In asking these questions, you're taking one of the first important steps toward growing your sales and revenue with a social media marketing campaign.

We've covered a lot of good ground designed to set you up for social media success. Let's revisit the key concepts and action steps and then move on to more good stuff:

- **Key concept**—The average tenure for a chief marketing officer is only 11 months.

- **Action step**—Avoid the fate of most CMOs by embracing the concept of running only social media programs that can be measured on an ROI basis.

- **Key concept**—Several basic formulas illustrate the impact marketing has on sales.

- **Action step**—Learn and understand the marketing mix formula outlined in this chapter. You'll be tested on it tomorrow. (We're kidding.)

- **Key concept**—Some larger corporations are using social media management platforms to manage their global social media campaigns.

- **Action step**—If you're a large global company, look into using Oracle Social, Socialbakers, or Webfluenz for social media management. If you're a small- to mid-sized company, try looking at SproutSocial, CrowdBooster, or Oktopost as an option for your company.

6

Why Your First Social Media Campaign Didn't Work

The vast majority of businesses use social media to connect with customers, yet only 12 percent can tie their efforts directly to revenue.[1] Why is that?

Why aren't 100 percent of those using social media tying it to revenue? Seriously, if you're spending $1 in business, it *has* to provide a return of $1 + X%. Otherwise, there's no point in making the investment. Even social media campaigns designed as customer service platforms essentially make money by either reducing churn or lowering costs.

Think of it this way—if you hired an employee and they cost you $50,000 per year, in some way, shape, or form, they have to earn your company $50,000 plus another $5,000 or $10,000 on top of that. Otherwise, there's no point in hiring them.

But most people running social media campaigns can't put their finger on whether or not the campaign is generating an ROI. In other words, social media is like an employee who costs them $50,000, but they don't know if that employee is generating $50,000 + X% in return or $50,000 − Y% in return. So, their social media campaign might be losing money for their organization—*but they have no way of knowing that for sure.*

Earlier in this book, we mentioned Red's Porch, the restaurant and bar that made one of the greatest offers of all time (free alcohol) to the first 100 people who followed them on Twitter. Unfortunately, the promotion didn't work. A number of factors contributed to the failure, but the main one was that Red's Porch didn't have social media magnetism.

If your brand has social media magnetism, it's so powerful that people are attracted to it the way metal is attracted to a magnet. People will go out of their way to be affiliated and associated with your company, because it gives them a sense of style, cache, and panache.

For example, check out MyStarbucksIdea.com. It's one of Starbucks' many social media campaigns, and it's a particularly good example of how Starbucks has leveraged people's passion about their coffee and turned it into brand loyalty. Brand loyalty is one of the components of social media magnetism. If you have it, as Starbucks does, you're golden.

The problem is that *you're not Starbucks* (unless, of course, you actually *are* Starbucks, in which case, we'd like to say, "Hello, Starbucks!").

Our point is this—if you're a company that sells paper or pet supplies or consulting services, you're going to have to reach out to consumers, stir things up a bit, and engage them in your social media campaign.

How can you do this? By creating a campaign that gives consumers something valuable that they don't currently have. This can be give-aways and other relatively traditional special promotions. This also can be information that the visitor finds useful. Better still, this can be a tool that keeps the visitor coming back for more.

TOOLS, TIPS, AND TECHNIQUES

Want to convert more website visitors into prospects or customers? Ian Cleary, founder of RazorSocial, recommends OptinMonster, which monitors mouse movements and, when a person is getting ready to leave your web page, drops a form in front of them encouraging them to buy your product or sign up for your e-newsletter.

One of the best and smartest versions of a tool that keeps people coming back for more is HubSpot's Marketing Grader tool. HubSpot has invested a great deal of time and money into their tool, which uses a sophisticated analytics engine to see how well your website is performing online. By sharing and promoting their Marketing Grader tool, HubSpot a) creates brand awareness, b) drives prospects to their website, and c) converts a percentage of those prospects to paying customers.

"A great way to get more customers using social media is not just to engage, but to *educate*," says HubSpot chief technology officer and co-founder Dharmesh Shah. "We believe in this passionately at HubSpot, and it has worked miracles for us. We've learned that the more people you *make smarter* by educating them, the more leads and customers you get."

So far, HubSpot's Marketing Grader has generated findings for more than five million URLs. So on more than five million occasions, potential customers for HubSpot have visited, engaged with, and interacted with their site. That kind of traffic is mind-boggling, especially if you're a company with only a few hundred employees.

Check out MyStarbucksIdea.com or Marketing.Grader.com the next time you're at a computer. You'll get a clear sense of what they're doing to engage people—and keep them engaged—with their companies.

This brings us back to one of the key questions a lot of folks are asking themselves right now: "If social media is such a powerful tool, why did my first campaign fail?"

It's a great question. We analyzed the most common mistakes people make when they run a social media campaign and came up with the following list. Read through it and put a check mark by the ones that apply to you. Don't be surprised if you have more than one check mark on the list—the idea is to figure out where you're coming up short so you can focus on fixing the problem areas as we move forward:

- *You didn't measure the results of your campaign.* Interestingly, this is an all-too-common problem. We discuss ways you can measure the results of your next campaign in Chapters 21, "Measuring the Quantitative Data," and 22, "Measuring the Qualitative Data."

- *You didn't set clear objectives.* Some companies create a Facebook page or a Google+ profile before they think through their objectives. Is it to build awareness? To drive traffic to a landing page on their site? To give people a channel to make comments and record their frustrations? When you start your campaign *with the end in mind*, you'll find you'll have better results.

- *You thought social media was only about Twitter, LinkedIn, Facebook, or Google+.* Of course, social media is about having many conversations across as many platforms as you can manage. The more opportunities you provide customers to engage with you, the more successful your campaign will be. That said, you'll want to resist the temptation to spread yourself across too many platforms. It's better to focus on one or two platforms first and have success there before moving on to additional platforms.

- *You didn't know how to set up a landing page.* One basic model of social media success looks like this: prospect → social media channel → landing page on website → new customer. If you don't have a landing page on your website that's designed to convert prospects to customers, it'll be difficult to track your return on investment (ROI). No ROI, no social media campaign (or, rather, no *effective* social media campaign).

- *You didn't remarket to customer prospects.* Most prospects who visit your landing page won't become customers. In fact, the vast majority won't. But that doesn't mean they're never going to buy. It just means they aren't going to buy at that time. Keep them in your pipeline—you'll get them someday if you remarket to them.

- *You didn't know how to turn a social media campaign into a sales and marketing campaign.* Social media isn't just about building awareness. It's about turning prospects into customers. Don't be shy about nudging prospects along the sales funnel. They expect it, to a certain degree, so it's a good idea to always nudge them along and continuously introduce them to your products and services.

- *You sat on the sidelines.* True story: We were in contact with a creative director at a major advertising agency many years ago who said, "This whole Internet thing is just a flash in the pan, and I can't wait for it to blow over." We're serious, he said that. Our point? You don't want to be that guy.

- *You downplayed the importance of social media.* Some people don't sit on the sidelines as much as they participate without passion. That's almost as bad as sitting on the sidelines. You don't want to be that guy, either.

- *You thought you could do social media in ten minutes a day.* Social media is a little like a marriage: You won't have a successful marriage if you plan on spending just ten minutes a day having a dialogue with your spouse. The same holds true for a successful social media campaign—it takes a consistent investment in order to make it work.

- *You thought social media was like traditional marketing.* Social media and traditional media have a lot of similarities, but they have a lot of differences, too. Your job is to embrace those differences and to leverage them for your business.

We could go on and on about some of the ways people's social media campaigns might have failed, but we won't. Our job here is to show you ways to *succeed* with social media, not how to fail.

So we'll keep going. But first, let's review the key concepts and action steps you should know from this chapter:

- **Key concept**—If you're serious about social media, you have to start formalizing the way you track and measure the results of your campaigns.

- **Action step**—The first thing to do is to start tracking key metrics on Facebook, Twitter, Google+, and other platforms. The second thing to do is to see if you notice any patterns or if you can derive any insights from what you're tracking. Later, we'll discuss some formulas you can use to take the data and actually calculate your ROI.

- **Key concept**—HubSpot and MyStarbucksIdea.com are two of the more successful models that companies are using to attract visitors to their websites.

- **Action step**—Visit both sites and study what makes these models successful. Use the sites as inspiration to do a bigger, better, bolder version of the same thing for your company.

- **Key concept**—Many businesses have launched social media campaigns but have struggled to make them work. Many of the reasons their campaigns didn't work are listed in the checklist in this chapter.

- **Action step**—Use our checklist to identify the areas you should improve on and focus on those areas in the future.

Endnote

1. http://www.emarketer.com/Article/Marketers-Still-Cant-Tie-Social-Bottom-Line/1009340

7

Managing the Conversation

Have you ever been in a situation where people were saying negative things about you? Maybe it was in the lunchroom in middle school or at a party when you were younger.

I f you're like most of us, you probably ignored the people who were saying the negative things. You probably let them continue their gossip and just walked away from them.

But what if you had decided to join the conversation? What if you had decided to introduce yourself and talk to the other people? What if you had decided that, once they got to know you, they probably wouldn't feel so negatively about you? If you had just taken a few steps and talked to them, they might have gotten to know you better and might have even changed their opinion about you. Who knows? They might have even said some *positive* things about you.

The same holds true with social media. If people are saying negative things about your company online, you have two choices. The first is to ignore the conversation. The second is to participate in it.

What happens if you ignore the conversation? Before long, others join in the fray and things quickly spin out of control. You end up reacting to the conversation rather than controlling it. That's not good.

Research indicates that when someone has a positive experience with your brand, that person might tell one or two other people about the experience. But when someone has a negative experience with your brand, that person will tell 11 other people about the experience. It's hard to say how many of the 11 people will perpetuate the negative story,

---

but it's safe to say that the "gossip" doesn't stop there. In all likelihood, an additional 10 or 15 people might hear the story from the original 11.

That's potentially 21 to 26 people who hear something negative about your brand, just based on one customer's less-than-stellar experience. But that research doesn't even factor in the power of the Internet, which can increase the effect tenfold or even a hundredfold.

DID YOU KNOW?

Information travels across the Internet at 186,000 miles per second, which is why companies have to work harder than ever to manage consumer sentiments about their brands.[1]

When Motrin ran a commercial about mothers who wear body-hugging slings for their children, several bloggers found it objectionable. Apparently, the bloggers felt that the spot took a swipe at mothers who have back pain as a result of wearing the baby slings. Messages like those seem to spread around the globe at the speed of light, so it wasn't long before the whole Motrin Moms commercial turned into the Motrin Moms fiasco.

A few days after the campaign launched, Motrin pulled the spot and issued a public apology. But an analysis conducted by Lightspeed Research found that almost 90 percent of the survey respondents had never seen the ad. When they did see it, about 45 percent liked it, 41 percent had no feelings about it, and only 15 percent didn't like it. Just 8 percent said it negatively affected their feelings about the brand, compared with 32 percent who said it made them like the brand more.

What happened? A handful of bloggers started a whirlwind of activity that resulted in so much negative content swirling around the Internet that Motrin had to cancel the spots—even though post-fiasco research indicated that the company didn't have to.

As mentioned previously, a similar incident happened to United Airlines when Dave Carroll uploaded "United Breaks Guitars" to YouTube. Dave wrote the song after United refused to pay for the guitar that some baggage handlers broke. According to U.K.'s *Times Online*, "within

---

four days of the song going online, the gathering thunderclouds of bad PR caused United Airlines' stock price to suffer a mid-flight stall, and it plunged by 10 percent, costing shareholders $180 million. Which, incidentally, would have bought Carroll more than 51,000 replacement guitars."

Whether Dave Carroll's YouTube video really was the sole reason the stock price dropped 10 percent is arguable, but the hard fact is that more than 13 million YouTube viewers now have a less than stellar impression of United Airlines.

It's easy to second-guess what United or Motrin should have done once things started spiraling out of control. But if they'd both been more deeply engaged in the online conversation—*if they'd both gotten out ahead of the story*—perhaps their situations would have been different.

Participating in the Conversation

So where does all this lead us? Right back to where we started: When you have a choice between participating in the conversation or sitting on the sidelines, you should *always participate in the conversation*. When you do so, you can help frame the issues and spread correct information about your brand or product.

Participating in or controlling the conversation is a little labor intensive, but sometimes you don't have a choice. We know a company based out of Atlanta, Georgia (we'll call them Brand A) that spends more than $15 million a year on traditional advertising. They're sophisticated marketers who track the results of every dollar they spend. They even track the online chatter about their brand and their competitor's brand online.

The problem is that Brand A is getting absolutely trashed online. Seriously, people are writing terrible (and usually false) things about their company. Worse still, people are confusing Brand A with a competitor who actually *is* guilty of some terrible things.

Yet here's the incredible part: Brand A has decided to sit on the sidelines and not participate in the conversation. Really? Are they nuts? Somehow these guys have decided that it's better to save their money than to invest it in reframing the online chatter that's damaging the long-term value of their brand. How's that for short-term, narrowly focused thinking?

So how do you manage the online conversation in such a way that people are exposed to accurate information about your brand? The starting point, of course, is to monitor the online chatter about your brand. You can use several companies to do this, including Socialbakers, SproutSocial, Oracle Social, and even HootSuite. Here's a quick rundown of what these companies can measure:

- **Raw data**—Online mentions across blogs, microblogs, message boards, wikis, social networks, video-sharing sites, and mainstream media.

- **Volume and trends**—Number of mentions across platforms along with an analysis of any important trends (either positive or negative).

- **Word analysis**—Insights to show what words are being used in association with your brand (such as *cheap, free, valuable, love,* and *hate*).

- **Competitive analysis**—Insights to show what words are being used in association with your competitor's brand.

- **Demographics**—Gender and age analysis of people describing your brand online.

- **Activity analysis**—Most active domains showing results for your brand (YouTube, Twitter, Wikipedia, and so on).

- **Geo-profiling**—Geographic distribution of posts about your brand, both nationally and internationally.

- **Sentiment analysis**—Positive and negative sentiments about your brand as well as noteworthy trends, either good or bad.

- **Forum comment metrics**—Analysis and insights around the comments and feedback in online forums.

- **Social platform analytics**—Demographic, geographic, and in some cases even psychographic information about your followers on different platforms.

But gathering data is just part of the challenge. The real question is, what are you going to do with the data?

One approach is to use something BKV Digital and Direct Response calls the i-Cubed system. BKV is a marketing communications firm that creates highly measurable marketing campaigns for brands such as AT&T, Six Flags, and the American Red Cross. (It's also the primary sponsor of the *60 Second Marketer*, the online magazine run by Jamie Turner, one of the authors of this book.)

When BKV saw the power and impact that social media was going to have on brands, it came up with the i-Cubed system:

- **Information** is all the data and statistics you can gather about your social media campaign. You can use several tools for this, in addition to the ones mentioned earlier, including Social Mention (very basic), BrandsEye, Sysomos, Social Radar, Brandwatch, and the old workhorse Google Analytics.

- **Insight** involves taking a deep dive into the data to explore patterns, spikes, relationships, and other information that you'll notice only after you've really digested the information. When you're investigating at this level, it's easy to get stuck in data overload, so don't be afraid to take a step back every once in a while and ask yourself, "Okay, I understand the data, but what does this mean in *human* terms? How can I translate this information into a story about my customers or prospects?"

- **Impact** is all about creating a campaign that leverages the information and insight and turns it into a specific, measurable, action-oriented program to drive revenue for your brand. If the data shows that long-form blog posts don't get much traffic, but your YouTube videos do, you'll want to leverage that insight into your campaign. (Of course, you'll want to go much deeper than that in your analysis, but you get our point.)

Using the i-Cubed System to Manage the Online Conversation

Not long ago, we used the i-Cubed system to help one of our clients navigate their way out of some highly charged and inaccurate information about their product, which was a sporting goods product. It's an interesting story and worth sharing because a lot of companies have probably had similar problems.

It all started about 15 years ago, when a product this company made malfunctioned. In almost all cases, the malfunction was the result of user error, but enough people were affected that lawsuits started flying around like a bunch of gnats on a summer evening. Instead of fighting the cases in court, the company decided to settle out of court.

The problem seemed to go away until, 15 years later, a little-known blogger decided to upload a poorly researched and inflammatory article post on his blog. The problem became pretty serious when Google ranked the negative post #2 on the first page of the search engine. The only site ranked higher than this blog post was the company's official website.

You can imagine the kinds of problems that raised for this company—a blogger with inaccurate information got ranked #2, which means that virtually every person who does a search around the company's products or brand name sees the inflammatory post. When you're in that spot, it's pretty important to do everything you can to fix the problem.

So what did we do? We used the i-Cubed system of Information, Insight, and Impact to develop a social media campaign that was designed to populate the Internet with accurate, transparent, and helpful information about the company. We pulled out all the stops, using YouTube, LinkedIn, Twitter, Facebook, Flickr, and seven different blogs designed to ethically, honestly, and transparently provide accurate information about the company and its products.

It's important to note that everything we did for this brand was aboveboard and transparent. Each and every blog we created identified the sponsor of the blog (our client). And we bent over backwards to avoid using any Black Hat techniques to try to manipulate results on Google. All we did was share accurate information about the product with as many people as we could in order to provide a more balanced and fair perspective on the reality of the situation.

What were the results? (Recall that the third *I* in the i-Cubed system is *Impact*, which means that you have to tie the results back to the bottom line.) The company dominated more than 65 percent of the conversation on the first page of Google. And by "dominate," we don't mean that the company flooded the Internet with sales pitches—that would have been counterproductive. Instead, we flooded the Internet with good, useful, and accurate information about the company's products and its industry.

Research indicates that more than 70% of the people who conduct a Google search don't get below the fold of the first page. If accurate information about *your* company and its products or services is below the fold—or, worse yet, on pages 2 to 2 million—then people aren't getting the full picture about your brand. If you find yourself in this position, be sure to take action quickly in order to manage the situation and fix the problem.

Several key concepts in this chapter are worth keeping in mind. But, remember, although it's important to understand the key concepts, it's even more important to put them into action. So keep track of which action steps you're going to implement and perhaps even let an accountability partner know about your goals so you can stay on course.

- **Key concept**—You have two choices in social media: ignore the online conversations about your brand or participate in them.

- **Action step**—Choose to participate in the conversations. Be helpful, friendly, and, most of all, accurate.

- **Key concept**—Dozens of companies can help you gather data about the online chatter about your company.

- **Action step**—Start gathering data related to this chatter. Many of the resources have free entry-level versions. More importantly, derive insights from the data so you can make adjustments and improve your campaigns.

- **Key concept**—The i-Cubed system is about information, insight, and impact.

- **Action step**—Make sure you follow this simple system in your next social media campaign. Gather information, develop insights, and track your results so you can measure the impact they have on your bottom line.

Endnote

1. www.fcc.gov/cgb/consumerfacts/highspeedinternet.html

8

Social Media Is More Than Just Facebook, LinkedIn, Google+, and Twitter

Social media is like a snowball. When it gets going, it builds and builds. With a little bit of luck and a good amount of work, your social media campaign will eventually create its own circular momentum. When that happens, you're off to the races.

The problem is that many people don't understand the concept of circular momentum. An effective social media campaign isn't just about uploading a YouTube video or creating a LinkedIn profile. It's about creating a wide variety of channels through which your customers and prospects can connect with you.

To a certain degree, the more channels you provide, the better the odds are you'll create enough circular momentum to generate real results for your campaign. We like to think of it as analogous to a house fire. (It's an odd analogy, but hang with us.) If your house caught on fire, you'd have two choices: 1) use your garden hose to fight the fire, or 2) call the fire department and use dozens of serious fire hoses.

If you decided to use the garden hose to put out your house fire, you might as well not even try. It won't work, so save your time and money. But if you decided to call the fire department, now you're talking. They can put some real effort behind the cause and, hopefully, save your house.

The same holds true for a social media campaign. If your idea of a social media campaign is to create a Twitter profile and then update it every day or so, don't bother. It'll never get the traction you're looking for, so it's not worth it.

But if you're serious about setting yourself up for social media success, put some serious effort behind it. Add some depth and breadth to your social media campaign. **Depth** is diving deep into each social media platform and really putting some energy into it. **Breadth** is doing social media across a wide variety of platforms, not just one or two.

This raises the question of how much bandwidth you have for additional assignments at work. How can you add responsibilities to your already-full plate and expect to do a good job with it?

The answer is that you'll probably have to segment some of your marketing budget for the costs associated with your social media campaign. Despite what you've heard, social media isn't free. Although some of the media costs are free (for example, it's free to upload a video to YouTube), other costs, such as the production costs and the labor costs, aren't free.

It's also important to really embrace the idea that social media is about more than uploading a YouTube video or creating a Facebook page. Sure, those are important components of most social media campaigns, but those are not the *only* components of a social media campaign. A good, solid, viable social media campaign crosses many platforms and requires a commitment of time, money, and focus for it to succeed.

TOOLS, TIPS, AND TECHNIQUES

Are you looking for a way to spread the social media workflow over a wide variety of employees? If so, check out EveryoneSocial, which turns employees into social broadcasters. This platform empowers employees to find engaging content to share with followers, or recommends articles and websites for them to share. EveryoneSocial is a great way to turn every employee into an ambassador for your company.

Social Media Tools to Help You Network, Promote, and Share

Okay, we've established that a good social media campaign is similar to a snowball that has the potential to build. We've also pointed out that a good social media campaign has depth (a serious, concerted effort behind it) and breadth (it extends across a wide variety of platforms). Now let's talk about the three broad categories of social media platforms—those that help you *network,* those that help you *promote,* and those that help you *share.*

Hundreds of different social media platforms exist, so we can't cover them all in this book. However, we can give you the most popular and relevant platforms that are part of each of these categories. By breaking them into categories, you can identify which tool is the most appropriate for your specific task.

You'll notice that you can apply some of the tools across several categories. For example, LinkedIn falls into the networking category, although it's often used to promote. For simplicity, we've assigned each tool to only one category.

We go into more depth on each of these tools in the upcoming chapters, but let's take a quick look at the tools that help you network. You can find a bunch of them if you look around, and the ones you're probably most familiar with include LinkedIn, Facebook, Google+, Pinterest, and Twitter, but the list doesn't stop there. Social/mobile tools such as Instagram, Vine, and Snapchat are also great tools you can use to connect with others on a professional (or more casual) level. Classmates and MyLife are tools that can help you find people who know you, and you can see who's searching for you. Ning and Socialcam are also excellent tools to help you share your life with others online.

MONEY-MAKING TIP

Social media isn't free. Both hard and soft costs are involved. It's important to include those costs in your metrics so that you can accurately measure your social media return on investment (ROI).

The social media tools that can help you *promote* are the tools that are often used for sales and marketing. You can use them to drive traffic to your website or to your social media channels. By doing so, you're using social media to do more than just build awareness—you're using it to drive revenue. And what's the point of doing anything in business if it doesn't ultimately drive revenue, right?

Some of the best-known social media tools you can use to help promote include YouTube, Pinterest, and Facebook. Other great social media promotional tools include Picasa (photo sharing and editing), Tumblr (blogging community), and Google+.

Using social media to promote your product or service is an art that we'll discuss in upcoming chapters, but realize that heavy-handed promotions can sometimes backfire. Social media is about *engagement* and *involvement.* The best way to engage and involve a prospect or customer is to soft-sell—give them something useful that they can use that will ultimately seal your relationship with them for a future sale.

As with romance, you have to build trust and engagement first. After you've built up some trust and engagement over the course of several dinners and a few bottles of wine, you can take your date home to meet your parents.

Tools that help you *share* are just as important as tools that help you network or promote. Sharing is a key activity for social media practitioners. When you share (information, how-to tips, and insights), you're building a relationship. And over time, that relationship can evolve from one that's about sharing to one that's about commerce.

The most familiar sharing tools include Instagram, Vine, and Snapchat, which are all tools that people use to share photos and videos with friends and family. But social media sharing tools go beyond those. They also include SlideShare (presentation sharing), Wikipedia (information sharing), and Yelp (user-generated reviews).

The bottom line about sharing tools is that they're an important component in any social media campaign, but they also take more time to gain traction. Because of that, many marketers focus on networking and promoting platforms before they get deeply involved in using sharing platforms for commerce.

What to Use When

Another important consideration is which tools are more relevant for business use (as opposed to personal use) and which tools need to be updated most frequently (resulting in a greater time investment).

The handy 2×2 matrix in Figure 8.1 outlines this concept. For our purposes, we're assuming that you're using social media tools to drive revenue, not to chat with friends. You can get some perspective on the tools that are more professional versus more casual, and the tools that require frequent updates.

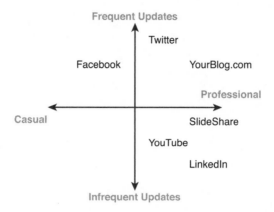

Figure 8.1 Using social media effectively involves understanding how to maximize the use of each platform.

LinkedIn doesn't usually require the kind of attention that Facebook requires, so you can "set it and forget it." Don't take that to mean you can forget about it for long stretches. It just means that you don't have to update it daily or hourly the way users update Facebook.

Twitter, of course, is the Mac Daddy of tools that require frequent updates. If you use it properly, you'll update it all day long, perhaps as many as 10 to 15 times a day. Remember, Twitter isn't about telling people that you're getting a cup of coffee or that the traffic was bad that morning. When used for our purposes, Twitter is about sharing information with your followers that they'll find helpful or useful. By sharing good information, you ensure that people will read and follow your tweets.

You can update YouTube whenever you have a new "how-to" video to upload. Remember, the reason to use YouTube for business is to provide people with video information they'll find useful. The best way to do this is to create videos that instruct and inform. With that in mind, you can update YouTube every week or every few weeks—whenever you have a new video to share.

> ## MONEY-MAKING TIP
>
> Data varies on this, but our experience indicates that search engines rank frequently updated blogs better than blogs that are updated infrequently. If you have a blog, try to update it two to five times a week.

If you have a corporate blog (and you should), you'll want to update it regularly. Uploading your best and smartest content to SlideShare is also an important task.

With all this in mind, let's cover the key concepts from this chapter and the recommended action steps:

- **Key concept**—Social media is similar to a snowball that keeps building—the more effort you put into it, the bigger it becomes.

- **Action step**—Don't think that you can do social media in ten minutes a day. A good social media campaign is an ongoing effort that requires regular attention.

- **Key concept**—Social media tools fall into three broad categories: those that help you network, those that help you promote, and those that help you share.

- **Action step**—Identify which platforms within each category will be most relevant to your prospects and customers. Make sure you use more than one or two platforms, but using more than 10 or 15 is probably overkill.

- **Key concept**—Some tools require frequent updating; others require infrequent updating.

- **Action step**—Be sure that you're aware of the workload associated with each tool before selecting it for your arsenal. Do a mental cost/benefit analysis of each tool before diving into it.

- **Key concept**—Some tools are more casual in nature; others are more professional.

- **Action step**—You want both casual and professional tools to be part of your social media campaign. A good balance of both gives prospects and customers a richer, more well-rounded experience with your brand.

9

Closing the Loop with E-mail and Marketing Automation

What is social media? Earlier in the book, we said it was a digital tool that allows you to have a two-way dialogue with prospects and customers. Based on that definition, aren't e-mail and marketing automation tools part of the social media family?

I n short, the answer is yes. Even though many people consider e-mail and marketing automation tools as a separate category, we consider them part of the social media family. Why? Because they're digital tools that allow you to have a conversation with your prospects and customers, and that's what social media is all about.

You're already familiar with e-mail because you get dozens or even hundreds of them a day. If you're not familiar with marketing automation, you can think of it as e-mail on steroids. In other words, it's e-mail marketing with a ton of bells and whistles that help you nurture leads and convert them from prospects to customers.

Both of these tools are important because social media tools such as LinkedIn, Facebook, Twitter, and Google+ are best for *establishing* relationships with prospects, but not as good at *converting* them. Oh sure, there are plenty of cases where social media is used to directly convert prospects into customers, but in many cases, social media is used as a branding and customer relationship management tool. In other words, it's used as a way to keep prospects engaged with your brand and involved in the conversation so you can convert them into customers later. The hard work—that is "the final mile"—is often completed via e-mail marketing or marketing automation.

The Final Mile

The typical approach for this involves using social media to engage prospects and to drive them to your website. That's the model used by the 60 Second Marketer, the blog for our marketing agency called 60 Second Communications. We use Twitter, Facebook, LinkedIn, Google+, Pinterest, and other tools to engage people and drive them back to the 60 Second Marketer blog, where we continue to remarket to them.

We often run A/B split tests to see which social media headlines drive the most clicks. By comparing two different headlines, we derive insights about our audience and, most importantly, improve our click-through rate (CTR).

In one A/B split test we conducted, we thought we had a winning headline when we asked our followers this question:

> "Want to learn how to calculate the ROI of a Social Media Campaign? We've written a free e-book on the topic...
> fb.me/laVnGwsi"

The CTR for that post was 1.17 percent, which exceeds the norms for a Twitter profile with more than 10,000 followers. (A study by Sign-Up.to found that the CTR on Twitter posts for people with 1,000 to 5,000 followers is 1.45 percent, but drops to 0.45 percent for people with more than 10,000 followers.[1])

As a side note, it's worth mentioning that generating a click is only half the battle. The other half is getting the visitor to convert on the other end of the click.

Conversion rates vary greatly depending on your business, so you'll want to compare your results to others in your industry. Typically something like a free e-book will have a 5 percent to 15 percent conversion rate on the back end. If you're selling something such as mobile phones, running shoes, or any other product or service, your conversion rate is going to be much, much lower—usually about 0.05 percent to 1.0 percent.[2]

No matter what your conversion rate is on the back end, you'll want to consistently test your way to success on the front end. In other words, you'll want to see which social media headlines drive the most clicks to your blog, landing page, or website. That involves split-testing headlines the way we did with the headline mentioned previously.

Here's the headline we tested for the second half of our A/B split test:

> "Learn how to calculate the ROI of a Social Media Campaign. Download this 20-page e-book from @AskJamieTurner: bit.ly/ HWaKKj"

How did the second headline compare to the first? We nearly doubled our CTR by writing a *definitive* headline rather than writing a *suggestive* headline. In other words, when we started the headline with the statement, "Learn how to calculate the ROI of a Social Media Campaign…," we had much better results than when we started the headline with "Want to learn how to calculate the ROI of a Social Media Campaign?" The first headline had a 1.17 percent CTR, whereas the second headline had a 2.18 percent CTR.

It's worth noting that we were intentionally testing two entirely different approaches to headlines. The second headline had a number of different variables, including the use of "@AskJamieTurner," which may have also contributed to the higher CTR. As you move forward with your own A/B split tests, you'll probably want to focus on one variable at a time. It's easier to identify what triggered the click-through when you zero in on only one change at a time.

A WORD ABOUT CONVERSION RATES

Conversion rates vary wildly, depending on what it is you're trying to accomplish. If you're offering a free e-book, you might expect 5 percent to 15 percent of your visitors to convert by downloading the e-book. But if you're selling something tangible, your conversion rate can range from 0.05 percent to 1.5 percent, depending on what it is you're selling.

As mentioned previously, driving a click to a landing page is only half the battle. Getting prospects to convert on the landing page is the other half of the battle. In some cases, you might be trying to sell a product or service. This could be just about anything, but would usually be something that you can sell via e-commerce. That said, in most cases, your intent is not to use social media to *sell* as much as you'll want to use it to *build relationships* with prospects who will be converted to customers later.

How would you do this?

The most effective approach is to provide something of value to the prospect that will introduce them to your products or services with as little friction as possible. **Friction** is anything that acts as a roadblock that would prevent the prospect from engaging with you.

A classic example of a high-friction offer is a free trial that requires submitting your credit card number in order to take advantage of the offer. That's serious friction and only works if there's a high-value product or service on the back end. In other words, if you're providing free 30-day access to an enterprise-scale, $1,500/month social media management system, then requiring a credit card for the free trial might work because the user is getting something worth $1,500/month for free for 30 days. But if you're selling a smaller $49/month social media management system, then asking for a credit card number is big-time friction and would vastly reduce your conversion rate on the back end.

One of the most common techniques to engage prospects is to offer them a free e-book, a free trial, a free webinar, or a software tool as a way to engage them with your brand. As mentioned earlier in the book, this approach was perfected by HubSpot, a company that has used this technique with great success. They call it "inbound marketing," which is also sometimes referred to as "content marketing."

No matter what you choose to call it, the approach is the same, which is to drive people to a landing page where they fill out a form in order to take advantage of the free offer. In the case of the 60 Second Marketer, one of our best-performing offers is for a free e-book called *83 Best Social Media and Mobile Marketing Tools for Business.* It was written by Erik Qualman, author of *Socialnomics, Digital Leader,* and other books, as well as Jamie Turner, the co-author of the book you're reading now.

What happens when people download *83 Best Social Media and Mobile Marketing Tools for Business*? As an "added bonus" for downloading the e-book, we also sign them up for our free e-newsletter. The e-newsletter comes out three to five times a week and alerts the members of the 60 Second Marketer community (also known as the 60 Second Nation) to the latest post on our blog.

The intent is to drive people back to our blog so that they stay engaged with the 60 Second brand. By staying engaged with our brand, several things happen:

- They eventually hire 60 Second Communications as their agency.

- They hire Jamie Turner or Reshma Shah to speak at an event.

- They use the 60 Second Marketer–sponsored e-mail program to advertise to our readers.

It's important that the blog provides enough free and interesting information that people want to keep coming back for more. We've tested nearly 1,000 different blog headlines over the course of our history. What are some of our most popular posts? Here goes:

- "The Truth About Social Media That Nobody Else Will Tell You."

- "I Was Shocked When I Learned About This Fatal Flaw in Word-Press Websites."

- "Forget Everything You've Learned About SEO and Do This One Thing Instead."

- "The 14 Most Powerful and Effective Words in Marketing."

You'll notice that the headlines are intentionally written to elicit an emotional response. In other words, we try to avoid news headlines such as "Facebook Launches New Update to Rave Reviews" and headlines that don't provide value, such as "60 Second Communications Hires New Employee."

Instead, we focus on topics that can provide *actionable* information for our audience that they can use to grow their own businesses. Just as importantly, we write thought-provoking headlines around those topics that drive clicks back to the blog.

Using E-mail Marketing and Marketing Automation to Close the Loop

Okay, so now you know how we use social media to engage people and drive them through to the 60 Second Marketer blog. You can use the same technique for your blog or website, too. But we still have an important issue to address—how do we close the loop? In other words, our ultimate goal is to engage people in a transaction of some sort, so how do we do that?

That's where e-mail marketing and marketing automation come in. These tools are designed to continuously drive prospects and customers back to your website. The benefit of doing this is that over time these prospects become advocates of your brand as well as your products or services.

As mentioned previously, the end game for the 60 Second Marketer blog is to get people to hire the agency (60 Second Communications), to hire Jamie Turner or Reshma Shah to speak at an event, or to advertise to members of the 60 Second Nation via our sponsored e-mail program.

This isn't blatantly obvious to the casual visitor to the blog because we don't want to do the hard sell early on. Instead, we build a relationship with them that elicits trust so that when they do find out about our products or services, they're more inclined to buy.

You can use a lot of different tools to accomplish the same thing, so let's take a look at some of these. Here's a quick rundown of some of the best-known e-mail service providers in the marketplace (we'll get to the marketing automation companies in a minute):

- **AWeber**—One of the better-respected e-mail service providers. These guys have strict guidelines in place for their customers that are designed to keep them whitelisted and off the dreaded SPAM blacklists.

- **Constant Contact**—Also well known and well respected. A good, solid contender in the marketplace. Constant Contact also runs events around the country designed to teach people about the benefits of e-mail marketing.

- **Emma**—Do you take great pride in your design and creative skills? Then Emma (found at MyEmma.com) might be right for you. Well-designed templates and a creative flair are what differentiate Emma from other e-mail service providers.

- **GetResponse**—More than 300,000 customers use GetResponse. Many of these customers include well-known brands such as Marriott, GlaxoSmithKlein, and *Men's Health* magazine. GetResponse is another well-respected provider.

- **iContact**—As part of the Vocus family of companies, iContact has a robust set of integrated tools that are specifically designed for small- to medium-sized businesses. If you're looking for a lot of bells and whistles without the added expense of marketing automation, then iContact may be just what you're looking for.

- **MailChimp**—How can you not love an e-mail service provider that uses a chimp as its mascot? Their clean, uncluttered web interface and their devotion to customer service are just two of the many reasons so many people put MailChimp high on the list of top e-mail service providers.

E-mail service providers like the ones listed are perfect for businesses that need simple, cost-effective tools designed to keep customers engaged with their brands. But if you're ready to take the next step up—that is, if you're ready to use an automated system with a lot of bells and whistles—then you might want to explore some of the marketing automation software providers mentioned next.

What's the primary difference between an e-mail service provider and a marketing automation software solution? Interestingly, to the recipient of the e-mail, there's not a lot of difference. Instead, it's what goes on behind the scenes that makes marketing automation software different from simple e-mail marketing software.

The easiest way to describe marketing automation software is to say that it's e-mail marketing that *thinks*. The software uses a set of logic and rules designed to send triggered e-mails to prospects at pre-determined times. Different e-mails are sent to different prospects depending on where they are in the sales funnel.

As an example, if someone clicks through on your e-newsletter once every six months, they'd probably be less interested in your products and services than someone who clicks through 20 times in six months, right? The person who clicks through 20 times is engaged with your brand and is showing their interest by visiting your website with some regularity. Marketing automation gives you the ability to tell where that 20-visit person is in the sales funnel and to send them specialized communications based on their behavior.

With all that in mind, let's take a look at some of the marketing automation companies you might want to consider if you're ready to take the next step up:

- **Act-On**—These guys focus on the "Fortune 5,000,000," which means they're perfect for the 99.99 percent of all businesses that aren't members of the Fortune 500. They're well respected and offer a simple-to-use platform that has everything most businesses need.

- **Eloqua**—Now part of the Oracle Marketing Cloud, Eloqua is one of the original members of the marketing automation industry. It's a clean, well-run platform that delivers the goods for many well-known brands around the globe.

- **ExactTarget**—Now part of Salesforce.com, ExactTarget is one of the best-known members of the marketing automation industry. They started out as an e-mail service provider and have buffed-up their offerings to the point where they're one of the more prominent members of the marketing automation space.

- **HubSpot**—Think of HubSpot as marketing automation software, plus a blogging platform, plus an analytics platform—all on steroids. HubSpot has done a great job updating their platform so that it continuously offers more and more options without becoming so complex as to be unusable.

- **InfusionSoft**—Best known for a visual campaign manager that lets you drag and drop your next campaign quickly and easily, InfusionSoft is used by more than 72,000 people around the globe. They have a good reputation and are the favorite of many thought leaders in the marketing industry.

- **LeadLife**—Founded by Richard Brock, one of the grandfathers of marketing automation, LeadLife is perfect for small- to mid-sized businesses interested in a seamless, easy-to-use platform. They also offer a "white list" version for agencies that want to offer an agency-branded marketing automation platform to their clients.

- **Marketo**—A very well-known marketing automation platform. Customers include Hyundai, the American Kennel Club, and Curves. Oh, and Harvard Business School uses them, too. Enough said.

- **Silverpop**—Recently acquired by IBM, this is a robust, full-featured platform that takes behavioral marketing to some new and interesting places.

We've covered a lot of ground over the previous pages, so let's do a quick recap and take a look at some important action steps:

- **Key concept**—E-mail marketing and marketing automation are digital tools that provide companies the ability to have a two-way dialogue with their prospects and customers.

- **Action step**—Make a decision about which tool is right for you—a simple e-mail marketing tool, or a more robust (and expensive) marketing automation tool.

- **Key concept**—E-mail marketing and marketing automation allow you to "close the loop" with your prospects and convert them to customers.

- **Action step**—Wrap your mind around the concept of lead nurturing, which is the process of having a digital conversation with your prospects. By having a dialogue with them, you can introduce your products and services to them gradually over time.

- **Key concept**—In the end, your goal is to convert prospects into customers.

- **Action step**—Start using e-mail marketing or marketing automation to drive subscribers back to your website. By doing so, you're building trust with them. When prospects trust you, many of them eventually become customers. Remember, if you're using social media for business, all roads should eventually lead to ROI.

Endnotes

1. http://www.mediabistro.com/alltwitter/twitter-ctr_b30416

2. http://www.searchmarketingstandard.com/what-is-the-average-conversion-rate

10

How to Use Networking Platforms to Help You Grow Your Sales and Revenue

*You're a farmer. That might come as a surprise to you,
especially if you're reading this from an apartment in New York
City or a Starbucks in Seattle. But the truth is that anybody
in business, whether it's a service business or a manufacturing
business, is also in the business of farming.*

W hy is this so? Because for any business to survive, it needs to have sales and revenues; and to have sales and revenues, you must have customers; and to have customers, you must have prospects.

How do you get prospects so that you can turn them into customers? We know of only one way to accomplish this: Plant the "business seeds" today so that you can have a plentiful harvest tomorrow.

If you're a real estate agent, a restaurant owner, or an interior designer, you have to connect with people *today* so that you have customers *tomorrow*.

If you're an accountant, a lawyer, or a dentist, you have to connect with people *today* so that you have customers *tomorrow*.

If you're a web designer, an architect, or a photographer, you have to connect with people *today* so that you have customers *tomorrow*.

If you sell cars, boats, motor homes, light fixtures, tools, food, knick-knacks, clothing, or CDs, you have to connect with people *today* so that you have customers *tomorrow*.

The bottom line is that we all have to plant seeds today so that we can harvest the fruits of our labor tomorrow. And if we don't plant seeds on a consistent basis, we end up not having enough customers down the road.

Here's some good news. Social media is the perfect tool for people who understand that what you're doing today will influence your success tomorrow. It's a great way for businesses (such as yours) to build relationships with people who will buy your product in the future. And by nurturing those relationships now, you're ensuring that you'll have plenty of customers later.

TOOLS, TIPS, AND TECHNIQUES

Want to monitor what your competition is doing online? If so, check out Rival IQ, which has an alert function that notifies you when one of your competitors has a social media post that's gotten an unusually high number of shares.

Who Uses Social Media?

How many businesses are using social media today so that they have customers tomorrow? According to one study, more than 70 percent of the Fortune 500 have a Facebook account and more than 77 percent have a Twitter profile.[1] Another study found that 81 percent of small- to mid-sized businesses use social media.[2]

But research also indicates that individuals and businesses are taking a broader look at the variety of platforms they can use to network via social media. As we've mentioned, social media is about more than just a handful of social media tools—it's about a broad range of tools all implemented within a well-thought-out strategy.

Let's take a closer look at some of the available networking platforms and the strengths and weaknesses of each. (Recall that we grouped social media platforms into three categories: those that help you *network,* those that help you *promote,* and those that help you *share.*) The list on the following pages is by no means exhaustive, but it should give you a sense of the top tools that are out there and how to use them for networking via social media.

- **Facebook**—Mark Zuckerberg started Facebook out of his dorm room for his fellow students at Harvard. Today, toddlers to grandmothers can be found on Facebook. Strengths: Widely adopted by large segments of the population. Weaknesses: Will the younger generation stay on Facebook once Grandma has "friended" them?

- **Google+**—This is the new kid on the block, but poses a serious threat to Facebook and other platforms. Why? Because it's just so darn easy to use—the clean, simple interface makes connecting with friends, family, and business associates a piece of cake. Google+ was the fastest-growing social network in history and looks as though it's here for the long run. Strengths: Ease of use and uncluttered environment. Weaknesses: Competition from other well-established social media platforms.

- **Friendster**—A way to stay connected with everything that's important to you—hobbies, interests, causes, business, and so on. Strengths: A simple web interface makes this easy to use. Weaknesses: Not as widely adopted as some other platform-runs. Might have peaked.

- **hi5**—This is a social networking platform that skews a little younger than LinkedIn. Members can play games, watch videos, flirt, give gifts, or just hang out. Strengths: It's a great alternative to MySpace and/or Facebook for the younger crowd. Weaknesses: It may not be the best social networking platform for business.

- **LinkedIn**—This is the Grand Pooh Bah of them all. They've been around since 2003, which, in social media terms, is also known as "since the beginning of time." Strengths: Everybody's on Linked In. Weaknesses: Most people have trouble knowing what to do with LinkedIn after they upload their business information.

- **MyLife**—A clean, simple site that helps people connect with family, friends, and other relationships. Over 750 million profiles. Strengths: The easy-to-use interface is one of the site's great strengths. Perfect if you're looking for an engaging, simple way to connect with old friends. Weaknesses: Not as widely adopted as some other sites.

- **Ning**—This site connects groups of people who are passionate about particular interests, topics, or hobbies. Also, it was co-founded by Marc Andreessen, who helped launch Netscape. Strengths: Great for connecting with others who are interested in your area of expertise. Weaknesses: The user interface is so simple and uncluttered that getting started can be confusing. But once you've figured it out, it can be a good tool.

- **Plaxo**—Currently hosts address books for more than 40 million people. Helps people stay in touch with "Pulse," which is a dashboard that lets you see what the people you know are sharing all over the Web. Strengths: Graphical user interface makes it easy to use. Weaknesses: It's not as widely adopted as some other platforms such as LinkedIn.

- **XING**—XING has more than 8 million subscribers worldwide. It has over 34,000 specialized groups and over 150,000 live networking events each year. Strengths: XING adds new developments to its platform on a regular basis. Weaknesses: Not as widely adopted as some other platforms such as LinkedIn.

Dive Right In

Okay, let's assume you're the kind of person who likes to dive right in to something once they learn about it. In other words, now that you've reviewed the social media networking tools, you're ready to get going with them. If that sounds like a plan, then take a look at the following Quick Start Guide and dive in.

HOW TO USE THE QUICK START GUIDE

The steps outlined in this Quick Start Guide provide a great way to get started with social media. But remember, a good social media campaign is executed with long-term goals in mind, not just short, quick hits such as these.

1. *Set your objectives.* Are you interested in driving traffic to your e-commerce site? Or are you interested in generating leads for your professional services business? Or perhaps you're interested in only building awareness for your organization. Figure all that out and then you're ready to move to step 2.

2. *Get inside the mind of your customers and prospects.* Don't launch any social media campaign without first thinking through why your customers and prospects are interested in connecting with you. What's in it for them? How is connecting with you in their best interest? What will they learn by connecting with you?

3. *Focus your initial energies on a handful of platforms.* Start by putting a company profile on LinkedIn. Then create a Facebook page. Follow that by creating a Twitter account—and perhaps a Google+ account. But don't do any of these things unless you will put some serious effort behind it. There's no point in setting up a social media profile of any kind unless you're going to use it.

4. *Drive people to your LinkedIn, Facebook, and Twitter channels.* Remember, a social media channel is similar to a television channel—it's your specific connection to your "viewers." If you're going to drive people to your channels, make sure they have a reason to go there. Will they be able to get helpful information or a white paper? Will they be able to participate in a sweepstakes or a promotion? Will they be directed to a blog post that helps them in some way?

5. *Repeat step 4.* We're serious. Don't move on until you've repeated step 4 and spent a good amount of energy driving people to your LinkedIn, Facebook, and Twitter channels.

6. *Upload content regularly.* Now that you've driven an initial batch of people to your newly uploaded channels, you need to continuously update them with new and interesting information. Remember, your goal is to build a long-term relationship with your customers and prospects, so be sure to upload information that answers their "What's in it for me?" question.

7. *Keep your initial channels running while you explore other platforms.* Don't move to other social networking channels until the first batch is running smoothly and you are continuously updating these platforms. After that happens, you can shift gears and start exploring some of the other platforms that help you network. Remember, the key is to build (or rebuild) relationships with people before you start doing the hard sell. But when the relationship is established, you can say, "Did I mention that I sell insurance?" or "Have you seen our new e-commerce site that sells premium coffee?"

Let's recap some of the key concepts and action steps from this chapter:

- **Key concept**—It doesn't matter whether you sell cars, insurance, healthcare equipment, or pencils—everybody in business is a *farmer*, because we all have to plant seeds today to reap a bountiful harvest tomorrow.

- **Action step**—Start the process of planting seeds today so you can grow your sales and revenues tomorrow.

- **Key concept**—Certain social media tools are specifically designed for networking. Some of these tools include LinkedIn, Facebook, Google+, and Twitter.

- **Action step**—Visit the websites of the social media networking tools that you're unfamiliar with (sites other than LinkedIn, Twitter, Google+, and Facebook). Go ahead, do it. It'll take only about five minutes to see what else is out there.

- **Key concept**—The social media networking Quick Start Guide outlined in this chapter gives you some ways to get started right away.

- **Action step**—If you're interested in jumping right in, go ahead and execute the Quick Start Guide in this chapter. But don't think that's all there is to it—a good social media program executes the campaign from a long-term, strategic standpoint. The Quick Start Guide is designed to get you up and running, but it's not the only thing you'll need to do for long-term success.

Endnotes

1. http://marketingland.com/fortune-500-companys-social-media-use-on-the-rise-52726

2. http://mashable.com/2014/02/13/linkedin-social-media-study/

11

How to Use Promoting Platforms to Help You Grow Your Sales and Revenue

What's the point of setting up, launching, and running a social media campaign if you can't use it to promote your product or service, right? After all, the big idea behind social media is that you can use it to create relationships with customers and prospects to get them to buy more stuff, for more money, more frequently.

With that in mind, let's take a look at the social media platforms that can help you promote your products or services. In the last chapter, we looked at the tools that can help you *network*. Now it's time to move on to the tools that can help you *promote* your brand.

Before we talk specifics, it might be a good idea to take a 30,000-foot view of the purpose of using social media to promote a product or service. The biggest mistake most people make is that they use social media the same way they've used traditional media. They think of social media as a tool designed to broadcast a monologue about a product or service. It's hard to believe that people are still using social media this way, but it's true.

The right way to use social media is to create a conversation with your prospects and customers. Conversations go back and forth, not just one way. So if you use WordPress to create a blog about your company, you'll need to encourage people to engage with you by leaving comments, tweeting about your posts, writing articles on their own blogs about your posts, and doing other things that create the circular momentum and the snowball effect we discussed in previous chapters.

Remember, the secret is to stir things up a bit. By stirring things up and generating buzz about your products and services, you're creating the kind of energy that snowballs into bigger and better things.

Let's take a quick look at some of the social media platforms that help you *promote* your product or service. This isn't an exhaustive list, but it'll help you get familiar with some of the better-known promotional tools under the social media umbrella:

- **Bing**—Bing, Google, and Yahoo! aren't technically social media platforms, but they are tools that can be used to promote your product or service, so we're including all three in this overview. The technique for using any search engine to promote your product or service is the same, so you'll want to optimize your website so that the search engines see it. By doing so, you'll drive traffic to your website from the people doing searches on specific topics. Strengths: Bing uses "intelligent search" to make searches even more relevant for the user. Weaknesses: It's fighting against Google, which is a tough battle.

- **Blogging platforms**—Blogging is one of the tools that could fit nicely in the *promotion* category or the *sharing* category. We've decided to include it in the promotion category because our ultimate objective is to grow your business, not simply share personal updates. A number of tools can be used to create blogs. Some of them, like Blogger, Tumblr, and Xanga, are straightforward platforms that are great for people who want to do a simple blog about their vacation, their company, or their family reunion. If you're ready to create a more robust blog that adds a lot of SEO value for your website, you'll want to use Joomla, Drupal, Typepad, or WordPress. These are the blogging platforms used by serious bloggers.

- **Discussion boards and forums**—Are you interested in creating an online forum where members of your community can engage with each other and offer each other advice? Then a discussion board or forum is for you. The best-known platforms for forums include Lefora, Zoho, Drupal, PhpBB, Simple Machines, Vanilla, JavaBB, and vBulletin. Strengths: Forums are a great way to build a relationship with customers and prospects. Weaknesses: They require regular, ongoing time and energy to keep them running properly.

- **Google**—Google is technically not a social media platform, but can be used as a social tool to drive visits to your well-optimized website. Strengths: Ease of use and pervasiveness. Weaknesses: Are they spreading their brand across too many channels? Does this confuse people? (Answer: Probably not, but we're struggling to come up with any weakness for Google. They're just so darn nice, it's hard to figure out what they're *not* good at. They're even good at not being evil, you know?)

- **E-mail marketing platforms**—E-mail can often get overlooked in the world of social media, but if you define social media as tools that help you have a dialogue with your customers and prospects, then e-mail falls into the social media category. Popular e-mail marketing tools include AWeber (affiliate link), Constant Contact, iContact, ExactTarget, and others. Strengths: E-mail is a highly measurable way to connect with customers and prospects. Weaknesses: E-mail marketing requires a concerted, ongoing effort if you're going to do it right.

- **Flickr**—This is a photo-sharing site that can be used to build awareness and drive traffic to your product pages. Whether you're selling hunting rifles or tennis rackets or widgets, you'll want to use Flickr to: a) build awareness for your product and b) drive people from Flickr to your website. Strengths: Flickr is easy to use and has a clean user interface. Weaknesses: Photo-sharing sites are important, but they're not the very first thing you'll want to work on in your social media campaign.

- **Howcast**—Wouldn't it be cool if there was a website where you could watch "How To" videos on the topic of your choice? Well, there is, and it's called Howcast. It's an extremely worthy competitor to YouTube. Strengths: A great place to upload high-quality content. Weaknesses: The default is still YouTube. Most people are conditioned to automatically type "YouTube" into their browser.

- **iTunes**—This is not the only podcasting site, but it's the best known and most popular. If you're doing interviews with industry experts or if you're creating mini radio shows, iTunes is the place to be. Strengths: It's a well-known, well-respected platform. Weaknesses: If you don't create scintillating content, people won't come back for more.

- **MySpace**—Ahhh, MySpace. They arguably started this whole social media thing to begin with. Today, MySpace is primarily used as a site for people interested in music and pop culture. Strengths: A well-known social media platform that most everybody has visited at one time or another. Weaknesses: It's really geared for people interested in music.

- **Picasa**—This is a photo-organizing, -editing, and -sharing site that's owned by Google. You can tag photos to enable quick searches by users. Strengths: As with most Google services, Picasa is easy to use and loads very quickly. Weaknesses: Photo sharing is important, but it's not the very first thing you'd want to work on in your social media campaign.

- **Twitter**—A surprisingly successful tool that is widely adopted and used for everything from business to fun and games. Strengths: Used by large segments of the population. Weaknesses: Can be a distraction, especially if you have Attention Deficit Disor... wow, look at that bird outside my window!

- **Vimeo**—Think of Vimeo as a high-end YouTube. It's perfect for people interested in sharing their videos with a community of positive, encouraging, creative professionals. Strengths: You gotta love a site that oozes upbeat, optimistic, life-affirming energy like Vimeo does. Weaknesses: It's not a default site the way YouTube is, but that may change in the near future.

- **Yahoo!**—Like Google and Bing, this is not technically a social media platform. But it is a tool that ultimately can drive traffic to your website. Be sure to optimize your website so that search engines such as Yahoo! can see it. Strengths: Yahoo! is one of the workhorses of the search engine world, so it's always a good idea to keep it on your radar screen. Weaknesses: Is Yahoo! a search engine? An online portal? A web magazine? Perhaps it's all of these things. And perhaps that's not a weakness after all.

- **YouTube**—Of course, YouTube is one of the better-known platforms used to promote businesses. The key to YouTube is to keep the videos short and sweet. Make sure they solve the "What's in it for me?" equation. YouTube is perfect for "how-to" videos, but it's not a good place to upload the CEO's annual speech to shareholders. Strengths: YouTube is ubiquitous. Weaknesses: It's a cluttered environment that can sometimes have some pretty racy videos on it. (Or so we've heard.)

That's a pretty straightforward review of the main platforms you can use to promote products or services via social media. The most common question coming out of an overview such as this is, "Where should I start?" The following Quick Start Guide can be used as a way to kick off your use of these social media promotion tools.

QUICK START GUIDE: READY TO DIVE IN? GREAT, LET'S GET GOING:

1. *Start by optimizing your existing website so that Google, Yahoo!, Bing, and other search engines can find it.* Use Marketing.Grader.com, Compete.com, or Alexa.com to compare your website's SEO visibility to your competitors' sites.

2. *Launch a blog.* The best and arguably most important way to drive traffic to your site is to launch a blog. WordPress, Drupal, Joomla, and Typepad are the most popular platforms for this.

3. *Upload new blog posts at least three times a week.* Make sure your blog headlines and your title tags are phrases people are likely to search on so that you get visibility on search engines.

4. *Create an e-mail newsletter.* Your customers and prospects want to be kept up to date on your latest special offers, right? Or they might want to read your white papers or articles that can help them with their businesses, correct? E-mail is one of the more important social media tools, and it's easy to implement. Don't ignore it.

5. *Upload content to Pinterest.* Even though Pinterest is also a shar-ing platform (discussed in the next chapter), many businesses are using it to promote their products and services. There's an art to using Pinterest for promotional purposes, but it can be a very effec-tive tool if used properly.

6. *Produce a short video.* This doesn't have to be a top-notch, profes-sional-quality video. It can be a basic video shot on a flip camera. The key is to provide content that's helpful and useful to your pros-pects and customers.

7. *Create a YouTube channel.* Don't just upload your video to You-Tube. Create your own channel so that you can customize the vid-eos and the user experience.

8. *Supercharge your promotional videos with TubeMogul.* This is a one-stop shop that distributes your video across many platforms, such as YouTube, Viddler, Howcast, Vimeo, and Metacafe. It's a great timesaver.

9. *Promote, promote, promote.* Use traditional media, word-of-mouth media, social media, and any other technique you can think of to promote the heck out of your blog, your YouTube channel, and your e-mail newsletter. After all, what's the point of doing all that work if nobody knows you're out there?

Let's recap a few of the key concepts and action steps in this chapter:

- **Key concept**—Social media is different from traditional media, because social media is about having a *dialogue,* not a *monologue.*

- **Action step**—Make sure all your social media campaigns are designed to build relationships with your customer prospects. Encourage comments, retweets, and Facebook posts.

- **Key concept**—Certain social media tools are great for promoting your products and services. These include user-generated videos, blogging, e-mail marketing, and other platforms mentioned in this chapter.

- **Action step**—Don't just talk about doing a video, a blog, or an e-mail campaign—do it!

- **Key concept**—The social media promotion Quick Start Guide outlined in this chapter gives you some ways to get started right away.

- **Action step**—Go ahead and execute the Quick Start ideas in this chapter. They're a quick, easy way to jump into the world of social media.

12

How to Use Sharing Platforms to Help You Grow Your Sales and Revenue

---

In the past few chapters, we've looked at social media platforms that can help you network and platforms that can help you promote. Now we'll look at social media platforms that can help you share information about your products and services.

Before we dive in to the specific sharing platforms, let's talk about what it actually means to share. We've already talked about the danger of over-promoting with your social media campaign. We mentioned that doing the hard sell using social media is usually counterproductive.

The reason for this is that social media is viewed (consciously or subconsciously) as a free tool on the Internet. In other words, people see blogs, forums, and communities as part of a web of interconnected dialogues that aren't necessarily intended for commerce.

Sure, people use the Web for commerce, but in many cases, people launch their web browser without the intent of buying anything. Therefore, they resent people who come on too strong with a sales pitch. They consider the social media world a safe haven from marketers and corporations trying to sell products and services.

TOOLS, TIPS, AND TECHNIQUES

SlideShare is a great social sharing tool. One SlideShare deck we created called "50 Amazing Facts about Mobile Marketing" received over 150,000 shares. So what did we do after that? We uploaded it again 12 months later and got another 92,000 shares. Remember, just because a SlideShare deck has been uploaded once doesn't mean it can't be uploaded again later.

Imagine that you're at a summer cocktail party. You've got a glass of wine in your hand, the breeze is blowing, and burgers and hot dogs are on the grill. Now imagine that someone walks over to you to strike up a conversation. That's harmless enough. But now imagine that the first thing they said to you was, "I've got a special deal on a sports cars right now. Let's talk monthly payments." That would be off-putting, right?

The same holds true for most (but not all) social media campaigns. In most cases, the last thing you want to do is to start selling right away. The first thing you want to do is to start a conversation, to get to know the person, and connect in a meaningful way.

We talked previously about how you want to approach social media as you do dating. You don't ask someone to marry you on your first date. Instead, you ask them questions about their interests and hobbies. If all goes well, at the end of the date, you ask them out for a second date. On the second date, you get to know them better and ask more personal questions. This, of course, leads to a relationship that, hopefully, moves to a third date, then a fourth, then... marriage!

We're kidding about the marriage thing (sort of), but you get our point. Social media and dating are very similar. The idea is to build a lasting, trusting relationship that will result in some sort of fulfilling relationship.

Given all that, let's take a look at social media platforms that you can use to share information about your product or service. Remember, these sharing platforms are designed to provide helpful tools, tips, or techniques to your prospects and customers. In other words, they're not necessarily used for the hard sell. They're best for building awareness, interest, and desire for your product or service. If you play your cards right, that will ultimately result in a business transaction.

Let's take a look at these platforms:

- **Buffer**—This social media management tool allows you to schedule tweets and Facebook updates quickly and easily from your web browser. It's perfect for people not interested in using TweetDeck or HootSuite. Just sign up, install it on your browser, and the next time you're at a web page you want to share, hit the Buffer button and schedule the post for sometime in the future. Strengths: An easy way to schedule updates on Twitter and Facebook. Weaknesses: Other platforms offer the same functionality.

- **Delicious**—This is a social bookmarking service owned by Yahoo!. When someone tags your article, video, or blog post with a Delicious bookmark, it's the equivalent of a "vote." The more votes you get, the more visibility your content has on the Delicious website. Strengths: It's everywhere. Weaknesses: You have to have a lot of traffic and a lot of votes to show up on the radar screen.

- **Digg**—Similar to Delicious in that people vote for articles, videos, and blog posts they like. If your content receives enough Diggs, it's promoted to the front page for millions of visitors to see. Strengths: Like Delicious, Digg is everywhere. Weaknesses: You have to have a lot of traffic and a lot of votes to show up on the radar screen.

- **HootSuite**—This isn't a social media platform as much as it's a tool that allows you to manage multiple social media channels through one dashboard. If you have a company with more than one contributor to your social media program, HootSuite is a good solution. Strengths: A very easy-to-use interface. Simple setup, yet still powerful. Weaknesses: If you're interested in doing more than just uploading posts, you might consider a more robust tool such as SproutSocial or Oktopost.

- **Instagram**—A surprisingly fun photo and video app that has been swept into the Facebook family. Install Instagram on your smartphone and the next time you want to engage with followers, send them a stylized photo or a short video. Strengths: A fun, easy-to-use app. Weaknesses: Other apps provide a similar experience.

- **MarketMeSuite**—This is a social media dashboard that's similar to HootSuite and TweetDeck. It's perfect for people who are interested in drilling down a little deeper than either HootSuite or TweetDeck allow you to do. You wouldn't want to use MarketMeSuite in addition to the others, but instead of. If you need a more in-depth experience, MarketMeSuite may be just what you need.

- **Path**—A location-based social sharing app that allows you to share photos, memories, music, thoughts, and other moments with friends in your social media circle. Strengths: A fun way to share your life journey with friends. Weaknesses: Heavy competition from entrenched competitors such as Facebook, Google+, and others.

- **Pinterest**—We live in a visual world, and Pinterest leverages that. Tired of reading long blog posts but still enjoy skimming through images that are worth 1,000 words? If so, then Pinterest is for you. Just visit the site, sign up, and start sharing images by repinning them to your profile. Strengths: A visually appealing way to share information with followers. Weaknesses: Competition from a wide variety of other social media platforms.

- **Quora**—This is the perfect place to go if you're interested in asking a question that requires an expert answer. Just type in a question you have about any topic and Quora will provide answers from other users. Quora is frequented by smart, well-educated users, so the answers tend to be very helpful and well thought out. Strengths: A simple, easy-to-use platform. Weaknesses: A simple Google search can sometimes offer the same quality of answers.

- **Reddit**—Similar to Digg and Delicious. Reddit is a source for what's new and popular on the Web. Users can vote articles up or down on the site, so readers can check out the hot, trending topics from blogs, newspapers, and other sources around the globe. Strengths: Like Digg and Delicious, Reddit is everywhere.

Weaknesses: You have to have a lot of traffic and a lot of votes to show up on the radar screen.

- **SlideShare**—One of the better-known places to upload your content for sharing with others. Take your PowerPoint, your e-book, your podcast, or just about any other content and share it with the SlideShare community. Strengths: SlideShare is a great way to get in front of a large number of visitors. Weaknesses: There are a lot of other people competing for the same eyeballs.

- **Snapchat**—Warning: This was originally invented as a sexting platform, so use it with caution. That said, it's evolving into a more robust tool, so it may be worth considering for business. Strengths: It's hip and popular, especially with the younger crowd. It can be used for flash deals, too (special, limited-time offers). Weaknesses: Tracking has to be done manually. And, as mentioned, it was originally invented for sexting.

- **StumbleUpon**—Very similar to Digg, Delicious, and Reddit. When you rate a website that you like using StumbleUpon, it's automatically shared with like-minded people. And it helps you find great sites your friends recommend. Strengths: Stumble-Upon helps spread your content to people not regularly exposed to your products and/or services. Weaknesses: Competes with several other well-established tools, such as Digg, Delicious, and Reddit.

- **TweetDeck**—Like HootSuite, TweetDeck provides a way to track many of your social media channels on one dashboard. It can be a timesaver and a productivity enhancer, assuming you're not easily distracted. Strengths: It's very easy to set up and get started. Weaknesses: Like all dashboard tools, it can lead to distractions for employees who are easily... Whoa! Is that a fly on the ceiling or just a speck of dust?

- **Wikipedia**—It still amazes us that this user-generated encyclopedia is run by just a few dozen employees (along with hundreds of thousands of contributors around the globe). It's a great tool for *legitimate* entries. Don't try to game the system by adding overly promotional posts. But if your entry will be helpful to the

Wikipedia community at large, have at it. Strengths: It's a great tool for uploading legitimate, helpful content about your product, service, or company. Weaknesses: If your target market is over the age of 40, they might struggle with Wikipedia's miniscule type.

- **Yelp**—This platform offers user-generated reviews on cool places to eat, shop, drink, relax, and play. Yelp has an augmented reality smartphone application that makes using it on the run a blast. Strengths: User-generated reviews are a great way for customers and prospects to find out about your business. Weaknesses: Some people try to game the system with faux reviews, but Yelp does a pretty good job of keeping those faux reviews at bay.

A Quick Start Guide for Sharing Platforms

Okay, that should give you a sense of the social media sharing platforms available to you. This isn't a complete list, but it should give you a quick overview.

So where do we go now? What can you do with all this information?

That's a bit of a challenge. The networking and promotional tools we mentioned previously are a little simpler to use and easier to get up and running, but it's not impossible. So let's take a look at the following Quick Start Guide.

QUICK START GUIDE

Let's dive right in and get started, shall we?

1. **Add social sharing buttons to your blog and your website.** Social sharing buttons are the little icons that click through to your social media channels. You don't want to add them to every page on your site—just the ones that have content that you want shared with the world-at-large such as your blog and home page.

2. **Upload content to Instagram, Pinterest, Vine, and other sharing sites.** By sharing photos and videos with others, you can build awareness for your personal brand and your company.

3. **Start using HootSuite, QuickSprout, Rignite, or any other social media dashboard to manage your social media accounts.** These tools can effectively manage conversations across a variety of channels. They're great timesavers as well.

4. **Continuously add content that others will pick up.** This includes writing blog posts that will provide helpful information to your prospects. It also includes creating enough buzz throughout your social media campaign to get picked up and seen by others.

That should do it for now. If you follow these steps, you should be able to gain some serious traction on the *sharing* side of the equation.

Okay, let's take a quick look at the key concepts and action steps from this chapter:

- **Key concept**—The Internet isn't a great place for the hard sell. People don't expect a hard sell online, and they resist companies or individuals who play that game.

- **Action step**—Practice the soft sell in just about everything you do online. Build trust and awareness first and then let the customer come to you, not the other way around.

- **Key concept**—Social media *sharing* platforms are good places to build awareness for your company. They're not necessarily effective channels for converting customers. Typically, that's done elsewhere, such as the landing page on your website.

- **Action step**—Use social media sharing platforms as awareness-building tools, not necessarily as direct-selling tools.

- **Key concept**—Social media sharing tools require regular, ongoing maintenance.

- **Action step**—You can't "set it and forget it" with social media sharing tools. You need to update content regularly so that you continuously build awareness for your product or service.

13

It's Not about Social *or* Mobile, It's about Social *and* Mobile

Eighty-four percent of mobile owners say they use their devices while watching TV to socialize with friends and surf the Web. Of those, more than one million a day use Twitter to comment on the programs they're watching.[1]

What does this point to? It points to the fact that the days of considering social and mobile as two separate items are over. There is no social *or* mobile. There's only social *and* mobile.

Here's another fact worth considering: Facebook has nearly a billion users who access the platform via a mobile device. Even more amazing is that the majority of Facebook's revenue comes from mobile ads. That's right—*Facebook makes more money off of mobile than they do off of desktop.*[2]

So, how can you use mobile to connect with your prospects and customers? The starting point is to wrap your mind around mobile marketing in general. By understanding the fundamentals of mobile marketing, it'll be easier to see how to use social *and* mobile to connect with your prospects and customers.

Let's start with a key fact—we're a nation of multiscreeners. In other words, we don't simply use TVs or computers or smartphones or tablets to gather information about products or services. Instead, we use TVs *and* computers *and* smartphones *and* tablets to gather information.

Given that, it's important that any mobile campaign integrate seamlessly into a larger marketing program. Traditionally, this meant that a mobile campaign would be reverse-engineered to fit back into the larger marketing program. In other words, businesses would develop their marketing campaigns and then insert a mobile marketing campaign into the larger program.

But a more sophisticated approach is to actually think *mobile first*. After all, in the very near future, the primary way your consumer will connect with your brand will be via mobile device. In other words, mobile should be the *foundation* of your marketing program, not an afterthought.

THE BIG IDEA

There's no such thing as social *or* mobile anymore. There's only social *and* mobile.

It's important to consider the environment your prospect will be in while using their mobile device. Will they be entering a restaurant and using their smartphone to check in on Facebook? Will they be using a tablet to tweet to friends while watching TV? Or will they be uploading a photo to Instagram while on vacation?

The likely result is that they'll use their mobile devices in all of the aforementioned scenarios and many, many more. After all, part of what makes mobile relevant is that people have their mobile devices with them virtually all the time. That includes while they're at the store, while they're watching TV, and while they're in the office.

So, it's your job as a marketer to engage them with your brand in a contextually relevant manner. In other words, it's your job to provide them with information about your brand that takes into consideration where they are at the time they're receiving your messages.

One of the biggest challenges for many marketers is that they don't have a sense of the tools that are part of the mobile toolbox. They might understand what a mobile website is and might even understand how it differs from a mobile app, but they still haven't had a chance to see all the tools at one time. In other words, they haven't explored each element to see how it might work with the other tools available to them.

Although new mobile tools are coming online with relative frequency, several are particularly important. What follows is a brief summary of each:

- **Mobile websites**—This is a simplified and streamlined version of your desktop website that has been designed to appeal to a mobile visitor who is using their smartphone or a tablet to connect with your brand. If someone reads a Facebook post from their smartphone and clicks through on the link, you want them to land on a mobile-optimized web page, not a desktop web page, so the starting point for any effective social/mobile campaign is a mobile-optimized website.

- **SMS and MMS**—Short Message Service and Multimedia Message Service are systems that enable brands to send texts or rich media (graphics, video, audio) to prospects and customers.

- **Mobile apps**—Not to be confused with mobile websites, these mini software programs reside in the smartphone or tablet and can be used by brands to provide information or e-commerce with prospects or customers. All of the major social media platforms have mobile apps. And some of them, such as Snapchat and Foursquare, are *mobile-only* social/mobile platforms.

- **QR codes**—These are the small checkered square icons you see on posters, ads, and other printed materials. Only 19 percent of the U.S. population has scanned a QR code,[3] so they've never really gained widespread adoption. Even so, some companies still use them quite effectively.

- **Mobile display ads**—These are also known as mobile banner ads and are a great way to drive new prospects to a mobile website. The CTR on mobile display ads is often 5 to 10 times greater than the CTR on desktop display ads.

- **Mobile paid search**—Identical to desktop paid search, except for the fact that it's customized for mobile. The largest and best-known players in this field are Google, Bing, and Yahoo!.

Any mobile device needs an operating system in order for it to work. A wide variety of operating systems are used around the globe, including Apple's iOS, Google's Android, RIM's BlackBerry, Nokia's Symbian, and Microsoft's Windows Phone.

The operating systems reside in smartphones that are designed and assembled by manufacturers. Manufacturers include companies such as HTC, Motorola, Samsung, HP, Apple, BlackBerry, and Nokia.

BlackBerry and Apple manufacture virtually all of the phones used in their operating systems. Google and Microsoft, on the other hand, purchase their phones from HTC, Motorola (now owned by Google), Samsung, and HP.

Remember, the manufacturer is different from the carrier. The four largest carriers in the United States are AT&T, Verizon, Sprint, and T-Mobile. Other carriers around the globe include Vodafone, Orange, China Mobile, and Idea Cellular.

WHERE DO PEOPLE USE SMARTPHONES?

Harris Interactive reports that 12 percent of smartphone owners have used their phones in the shower and that 9 percent have used them during sex.[4]

One of the better features about mobile marketing is that the opportunities to target prospects and customers are very robust. You can target based on demographics, behaviors, location, previous websites visited, interests, and other techniques.

The starting point for any successful campaign is to define the demographics of the target audience. This typically includes age, education, and household income (HHI) but can also include overlays such as geographic location and ethnicity. Targeting based on demographic information is relatively simple for mobile marketers.

Behavioral targeting enables mobile marketers to target consumers based on real-world actions and behaviors. So, for example, a business can target consumers who have visited a sports website as well as an automobile website. Or, they can target consumers who have a preference for fine wines and international travel. The possibilities for targeting based on behaviors is virtually endless.

Retargeting is also one of the more robust aspects of mobile marketing. This enables marketers and app developers to retarget consumers who have visited their websites or downloaded their apps. It's a great way to convert an interested prospect into a happy customer.

In some cases, you may want to target consumers based on the characteristics of their mobile device and connection. For example, you may want to send different marketing messages to owners of AT&T, Verizon, Sprint, and T-Mobile devices. If that's the case, no problem—you can do that with mobile.

In other cases, you may want to connect with consumers at a specific time or place. That's a perfect opportunity to incorporate contextual advertising into your mobile marketing mix. Contextual advertising includes dayparting (for example, deploying the ad at a specific time of day) and situational targeting (for example, at an airport or an event), which works toward making the message that much more relevant and appropriate.

Finally, you may want to connect with consumers at a time when they're engaging with mobile websites or apps that are related to your industry. So, for example, if you manufacture golf clubs, sending a mobile marketing message to someone reading an article on the Golf.com mobile website is a no-brainer. Or, you can engage with someone who is using an app that's related to your product or service—for example, a winery might be interested in running ads in apps targeting wine and food lovers.

LEVERAGING CROSS-SCREEN TV VIEWING

Hawaii-Five-O was the first TV show to allow viewers to use social media to vote on the ending of a show in real time. CBS tracked hashtag votes during the episode and changed the ending based on viewer's preferences.[5]

Research indicates that the redemption rate for mobile coupons is ten times that of traditional coupons.[6] Part of this is because of the novelty of mobile, and part of it is because of the ability for mobile to be customized to be more relevant for the consumer.

For example, a geo-targeted display campaign that incorporates the user's location into the ad will almost always outperform a display campaign that doesn't reference the user's location. And a campaign using response codes such as QR codes has an innate ability to engage users because the process of scanning a code opens the door for other, more involved transactions.

What about mobile paid search? That's another great tool you can use to connect with prospects and customers. Keyword prices are still relatively low, so the possibility of having a positive ROI for a mobile search campaign is significant.

Starwood Hotels uses click-to-call mobile paid search campaigns that now drive the majority of mobile bookings for the chain. The ads use geo-locational technology to target prospects who are conducting searches near their hotels. The click-to-call numbers are delivered to the prospect's smartphone and include a map to the nearest Starwood Hotel. The result was that mobile paid search ROI increased by 20 percent, mobile bookings increased by 20 percent, and mobile traffic tripled during the course of the campaign.

There are a number of key metrics to keep track of when running and managing a mobile paid search campaign. A study by Marin Software found that consumers are more likely to engage with search ads on mobile devices than on desktops. In their study, the average CTR on smartphones and tablets was respectively 64 percent and 18 percent higher than the average desktop CTR.[7]

Keeping an eye on your average position is another relatively important consideration. On a regular paid search campaign, up to 11 ads are shown on any given page, but on mobile devices, only two or three appear.

Google also uses a quality score to calculate how relevant your ad is to searchers. The quality score is based on a number of factors, ranging from click-through rate to time spent on the landing page. The higher your quality score, the more effective your campaign. A way to keep your quality score in good standing is to include mobile-related keywords in your search terms. So, for example, include the term "locations" (for example, "Italian restaurant locations"), addresses (for example, "Home Depot on 42nd Street"), and ZIP Codes in your keyword search terms.

MOBILE PAID SEARCH LEADS TO ACTION

According to a study by Microsoft, 70 percent of all mobile searches lead to action within one hour.[8] Why? Because people who do mobile searches are already "out and about" looking for solutions to their problems.

Okay, now that we've done a quick spin through the world of mobile, it's time to get into the world of social/mobile. More specifically, how can you use social *and* mobile to connect with prospects and customers.

Let's start with the basics. You can kick things off by logging in to Linked In or Google+ from your smartphone and sharing a business insight while you're away from the office. It sounds simple—and it is—but you'd be surprised how many people haven't done this. So give it a shot.

For example, if you're in New York on business and are inspired by some of the innovative marketing concepts you see in Times Square, then share your observations with your followers. It's a great way to position yourself as a thought leader and an innovator. (Remember, an added benefit of using social/mobile is that it helps your clients know that you're a professional who is on the front end of new and innovative marketing tools.)

Alternatively, you can use promoted posts on LinkedIn that incorporate native advertising into the comment stream. The cost for doing this is $20,000 a month or more, so it's only for major brands, but it's an effective way to connect with high-value prospects who are viewing LinkedIn via their mobile devices.

One of the biggest challenges with mobile display (banner) ads is getting people to convert. Why? Because people don't want to fill out forms on a smartphone. What's the solution? Add a click-to-call button instead and give them the option of calling your company or sales force in order to complete the order.

Let's keep going. Did you know that Twitter not only lets you create promoted posts but also lets you choose which devices to target? That's right, you can create a promoted post campaign on Twitter that only targets mobile devices. Or, you can create one that only targets iPhones, or Android devices, or other smartphones.

The bottom line is that Twitter isn't just a desktop advertising platform any more. It's much more robust than that. And if you're interested in getting into the world of social/mobile quickly, then running a Twitter-promoted post just for mobile is a great place to start.

As mentioned earlier, Facebook generates more than half of its revenue from mobile ads, so why not jump into the fray? Initially, companies running ads on Facebook did so via desktop and mobile, almost using them as one and the same. But the number of advertisers running mobile-only campaigns recently increased 45 percent year-over-year.[9] Why did many of them go exclusively to mobile? Because mobile-only newsfeed ads have a 187 percent higher click-through rate and a 22 percent lower cost-per-click than desktop ads.[10] What's not to love about that?

Once you've leveraged LinkedIn, Twitter, and Facebook via mobile, you can move on to other platforms. Two of these include Instagram and Vine. Here are some tips on how to leverage these fast-growing social/mobile platforms for your business:

- **Find creative images or videos that promote your brand**—Post photos or videos of events, employees, your office, your products and services (both staged and in everyday situations), along with other things that provide an exclusive glimpse into your brand.

You can create images to announce upcoming releases, events, or contests.

- **Optimize the caption for searches**—Like other networks, Instagram and Vine use hashtags to identify topical association and help users search for photos and videos of interest to them. Avoid overloading the caption with hashtags, but be thorough to ensure that potential customers can find you in search results. Consider adding shortened links to your captions to point followers back to your website or to a specific page or post related to the photo.

- **Share**—You can post photos and videos from Instagram and Vine to Facebook, Twitter, and other networks by simply selecting them just before you publish your picture or video.

- **Interact with the community**—Make sure you're following current and potential customers. Like and comment on their photos as you see fit. Consider creating a hashtag for your company or blog (for example: #60SecondMarketer) to help monitor mentions and encourage participation. Share photos of customers at events. As with other social networks, social interaction should be the primary goal, which helps personify your brand.

Now that you've got a handle on how to use tools such as LinkedIn, Twitter, Facebook, Instagram, and Vine via mobile, you're ready to stretch your wings. Here are few other social/mobile tools that should be in your toolshed:

- **Scoutmob**—This is a deal-of-the-day site that provides local offers, many via mobile.

- **SCVNGR**—This social/mobile platform provides local offers via a scavenger hunt game.

- **Zagat**—This is a restaurant review site owned by Google. Check out their mobile advertising platform to see how to leverage it for social/mobile.

- **TripAdvisor**—Own a hotel, restaurant, bar, or other travel-related business? You can use TripAdvisor to market your business. Just let them know you want to run an ad that targets mobile devices and you can go from there.

- **Snapchat**—Even though Snapchat was originally designed for sexting, there are still some innovative uses of this platform as long as you don't think your customers or clients will be offended. But if you're a company such as Virgin Airlines or SPANX, you could have a lot of fun with this platform while staying true to your edgy brand image.

We've covered some important things in this chapter, so let's take a look at the key concepts and action steps:

- **Key concept**—There's no such thing as social *or* mobile, there's only social *and* mobile.

- **Action step**—Start taking a mobile-first approach to your marketing strategy. In other words, don't include mobile as an afterthought. Instead, lead with mobile.

- **Key concept**—Before diving into the world of social/mobile, it helps to understand the tools in the mobile toolbox.

- **Action step**—Review the tools outlined in this chapter. How many of them are you actively using for your marketing program? Are there any you can implement quickly and easily (for example, mobile paid search, QR codes, and so on)? If so, try to incorporate them into your next campaign.

- **Key concept**—Most social media platforms can be easily leveraged via mobile.

- **Action step**—It's easy to get started using LinkedIn, Twitter, Facebook, Instagram, and other social/mobile platforms. What are you waiting for? Dive right in—it won't hurt!

Endnotes

1. http://www.nielsen.com/us/en/newswire/2014/whats-empowering-the-new-digital-consumer.html

2. http://venturebeat.com/2014/01/29/facebooks-mobile-moment-nearly-a-billion-mobile-users-majority-of-revenue-from-mobile/

3. http://60secondmarketer.com/blog/2013/10/27/why-qr-codes-are-dead/

4. http://www.jumio.com/2013/07/americans-cant-put-down-their-smartphones-even-during-sex/

5. http://www.deadline.com/2013/01/episode-of-cbs-hawaii-five-0-lets-viewers-choose-ending-in-real-time/

6. http://blog.funmobility.com/2013/10/11/why-mobile-coupons-have-10x-higher-redemption-rate-than-traditional-coupons/

7. http://www.marinsoftware.com/resources/news/mobile-on-pace-to-surpass-desktop-paid-search-on-google-by-end-of-2015

8. http://www.mobilemarketer.com/cms/opinion/columns/8188.html

9. http://marketingland.com/4-top-facebook-advertising-trends-and-the-stats-behind-them-68462

10. Ibid.

14

How to Integrate Social Media into Your Marketing Plan

What do Geico and Shane Company have in common? They're both well-known brands that have made their mark with clever, catchy advertisements. But they also share a less flattering accolade that binds them together: They have largely failed to integrate their communications campaigns with strong, long-lasting brand messages that resonate with customers over time.

Tom Shane's commercial narrations for Shane Company, his chain of jewelry stores, left people wondering whether the brand could truly deliver on its promise to be their "friend in the diamond business." It wasn't until people actually went to the stores that they believed the premise: a store full of friendly, knowledgeable salespeople selling one-of-a-kind pieces at a good value. If you just relied on Tom's voice over the radio, you might not even wander into a store. And that's perhaps one of the reasons the company filed for bankruptcy protection.

TOOLS, TIPS, AND TECHNIQUES

Don't confuse a marketing campaign's *popularity* with its actual *success*. For a campaign to be truly successful, it has to be popular with consumers *and* make the cash register ring.

Sure, Geico has the lizard. And some love the lizard. But they also have the cavemen, the B-list celebrities versus real people, good news versus bad news vignettes, talking pot holes and parking lot columns, stacks of money with googly eyes, and a narrating spokesperson who reveals "truths" that are hard to believe. Who are they trying to reach? What's Geico's brand message? What if I don't like lizards? Although Geico is certainly gaining people's attention, the company has witnessed a lot of customer churn, which means that customers who buy their insurance often switch to another insurance company a short time later.

So even though their TV commercials may have been memorable, both Geico and Shane Company have struggled to retain customers over time. And isn't retaining customers the main goal of any marketing effort? It's not just about acquiring customers; it's about keeping customers loyal to your brand. Similar to a master chef who has a long waiting list for his restaurant, a successful marketer has to be skilled in mixing the marketing elements—product, price, place, and promotion—in such a way that customers keep coming back for more.

After all, consumers' perceptions of a company or a brand are the synthesis of a bundle of messages received via ads, packaging, direct marketing efforts, publicity, word of mouth, sales promotions, point-of-purchase displays, and even the type of store where a brand is sold. Most of these messages are marketer-generated, brand-oriented communications. Add to that all the conversations about the brand happening in social media. Clearly, brand messages can become garbled, diluted, or wrongly interpreted if they are being developed and disseminated in silos.

TOOLS, TIPS, AND TECHNIQUES

Social media optimization is the act of using a social media tool to send a single post to a variety of platforms. It's semi-controversial because it leans toward using social media as a *broadcast* tool instead of a *relationship* tool. If you can get past that, then you might check out Friends+Me, which enables you to post your Google+ posts to Twitter, LinkedIn, Facebook, and Tumblr all at once.

The Advent of Integrated Marketing Communications

During the early 1990s, companies began to realize the need for more integration across all of their promotion tools. These firms began moving toward *integrated marketing communications* (IMC), which involves making your marketing communications consistent, coordinated, and synergistic by ensuring that you're speaking with one voice across all communications platforms. You want to be sure that what the consumer sees and hears isn't a bunch of unrelated, confusing, and mixed messages.

A few other factors were driving the push toward more integration:

- Marketers were under pressure to show a return on their marketing dollars invested. Others in the organization felt that traditional media advertising had become too expensive and wasn't cost-effective.

- Media fragmentation had resulted in more emphasis on targeted media and less emphasis on mass media.

- Power was shifting from manufacturers to retailers, who had more information about end users. Many marketers shifted their focus to promotional tools, such as sales promotions, that could produce short-term results.

As marketers embraced the concept of IMC, they began to ask their ad agencies to coordinate the use of a variety of promotional tools such as public relations (PR), sales promotions, direct marketing, Internet, and traditional media advertising. Now we're seeing the need for integration all over again. Marketing executives are struggling to figure out how to keep their agencies coordinated as a slew of specialized digital agencies vie for their attention.

Moreover, today's efforts to integrate across the various marketing disciplines are much more complex, given the rapid advances in digital platforms and explosive proliferation of user-generated content. New communications and information technology compete with existing traditional communications forms. So integration is not just needed

---

across existing media forms; it's also needed across *old and new media forms.*

Don Schultz, Professor Emeritus at the Medill School of Communications at Northwestern University, developed a framework to illustrate today's marketplace as one of "push" and "pull" (see Figure 14.1). Marketers continue to push their communications out to customers and prospects through traditional forms such as TV, newspapers, magazines, radio, outdoor advertising, sales promotion, and PR. At the same time, customers have the ability to access, or pull, information from the marketer and the marketplace.

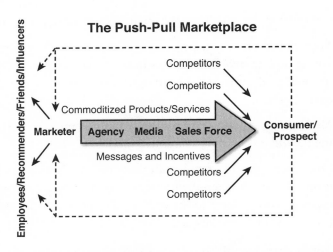

Figure 14.1 This framework, developed by Don Shultz at Northwestern University, illustrates the push–pull marketplace.

The primary change these new pull systems create is that customers are engaging in conversations about companies and brands around the world, often without the knowledge of the marketer. Control over communications has changed hands. What was once the sole domain of the marketer, to push out carefully designed communications about companies and brands, has now become the domain of all the players in the value chain.

The New World of Marketing

In this new world of push-and-pull marketing, marketers no longer have the power to simply push out specific messages. Aligning and integrating both push and pull communication formats is vital to success.

Given all that, who is ultimately responsible for managing integration—a business client or its marketing agency? Lead agencies bundled together with support agencies under large holding company umbrellas claim they should be in charge of integration. But clients believe that *they* should be in charge.

In a recent Forrester study of marketing and agency executives, called "The Future of Agency Relationships," researchers found that, over the past few years, the already-complex agency-marketer relationship has been significantly altered by factors such as the rise of social media. This has resulted in agencies quickly trying to expand their offerings, sometimes promising capabilities they are unable to deliver.

Sean Corcoran, an analyst at Forrester and lead author of the report, said one of the biggest challenges marketers face today is how to know who to turn to when they want to change their ad strategies to include new media. He said it's further complicated by the fact that the unbundled world of traditional, PR, interactive, media, and direct agencies are trying to "bundle themselves back up" to become jacks-of-all-trades.

THE BIG IDEA

The world of marketing is getting more complex. Today, the agency, the corporation, the retailer, and the consumer all have a say in the brand's positioning.

Regardless of your lineup of agencies, as a marketer, you are ultimately responsible for managing integrated communications for your brand. If you abdicate that responsibility, you run the risk of having your brand become diluted. Even worse, just as the managers for many brands have learned the hard way, customers might come away with entirely wrong perceptions about the meaning of your brand. Let's not forget Geico and Shane Company.

Outside of agency specialists, marketers are also dabbling with how to incorporate social media into their marketing plans themselves. Some have been experimenting with different types of social media platforms for the past several years; others are just now beginning to understand the true value that adding social media to their overall promotional mix brings.

Despite an organization's experience with and tenure using social media, marketers overwhelmingly are learning that social media programs are more effective when they are strategically integrated into the marketing mix than when they are used as standalone tactics. According to Michael and George Belch, the co-authors of *Advertising and Promotion: An Integrated Marketing Communications Approach* (one of the top-selling textbooks on the topic of integration), developing campaigns that integrate social media elements into traditional campaigns is the biggest challenge facing marketers.

Integrating Your Social Media Campaign

Anyone can create a Facebook or Twitter page. However, what some have failed to recognize is that not only do those pages need to be maintained with relevant, worthwhile content, but they also need to meticulously mimic what the company is saying in all other media. Social media can't be considered just an add-on or an afterthought just because others are using it. It has to be strategically integrated with all of your marketing communications, *even if that means starting fresh with a new approach.*

The most important issue is to establish a clear and consistent relationship between the social media you use and your traditional marketing efforts. A blog, for example, is a great way to get attention from your customers. When you have a potential customer's attention, it's time to funnel that person into your existing marketing model. Similarly, your Facebook page should contain the bare essentials of your marketing message and provide incentive for potential customers to visit your own website, walk through the doors of your business, or call and order a product. Driving fans to your Facebook page will do little for you if you can't then convert those fans into customers.

We've covered a lot of important topics in this chapter, so before we move on, let's take a quick look at the key concepts and action steps outlined in the previous pages:

- **Key concept**—Some brands have largely failed to integrate their communications campaigns with strong, long-lasting brand messages that resonate with customers over time, regardless of the touchpoint.

- **Action step**—Study the best practices of highly successful branding campaigns, such as those created for Chick-fil-A, Nike, and Apple.

- **Key concept**—Ultimately, your social media marketing strategies need to follow the same guiding principles as your other traditional marketing efforts.

- **Action step**—Keep your social media efforts narrowly focused on your target market, and try to use social media in a way that reflects your business's overall approach to integrated marketing communications.

- **Key concept**—Push-and-pull communications are here to stay. Marketers must align both forms in such a way that customers see the message as holistic, consistent, and originating from one source.

- **Action step**—Determine who will be responsible for managing marketing integration for your company and brand, and ensure that social media marketing efforts result in communications that are consistent with those of other vehicles.

15

How to Conduct a
Competitive Assessment

Wouldn't it be great if Coke had to worry about only Pepsi? Or if Hertz had to watch out for only Avis? And life would be simple if HP was concerned only about Apple. But that's far from reality. In most businesses, competition comes not only from your direct competitors, but also from indirect, industry-specific, and generic competitors.

s marketers develop their go-to-market strategies, they have to consider not only what their product or service has to offer, but also what their competitor's products or services have to offer.

The same principle applies when you think about your approach to an integrated social media campaign. It's important to start with a competitive assessment of your competitors' campaigns. Do they have a Facebook page? Are they Twitter aficionados? Do they blog like nobody's business? But it goes beyond that—you'll also want to analyze what they're doing *right*, what they might be doing *wrong*, and how you can do things differently to stand out.

Conducting a Competitive Assessment for Your Business

Before we start talking about how a competitor's social media strategy can impact or influence your own, it's worth looking at how competition in business works. For example, book retailers such as Barnes &

Noble and Books-a-Million have been facing disruption in their industries brought on by changes in technology and consumer buying habits. Just a few years ago, both retail brands were competing to see who could gain the most market-share.

While these massive bookstore chains were battling for physical retail dominance, an online empire called Amazon.com was being built with an almost unlimited selection of books. Today, Barnes & Noble and Books-a-Million are playing catch-up to boost their own website traffic, in addition to managing their bricks-and-mortar locations.

The point is that competitive myopia, a focus on current competition and existing business models, can actually render a business extinct. For example, if Coke thinks that its only competition is Pepsi, then it's missing out on both opportunities and threats. Coke is most often consumed to satisfy thirst. However, other common reasons to drink a Coke include to feel revived or energized, to escape boredom, for a sugar fix, and for refreshment, along with a whole host of other reasons.

Who exactly competes with Coke in all these areas? Take a look at the concentric circles in Figure 15.1, which explores the competitive frames for both the soda industry and the cruise line industry. In the Coca-Cola example, the soda competes with other cola brands such as Pepsi and RC Cola. At the next level of competition, Coke competes with other beverages, including water, juice, tea, and coffee, to quench thirst. At still another level, Coke competes at the level of providing satisfaction to the tired consumer, the bored consumer, or the consumer who just plain wants to drink something instead of eating.

At the broadest level, Coke competes with anything else that consumers could buy for the same amount of money they could spend on a Coke. Competition for dollars and the opportunity cost of using money to buy a Coke is the broadest form of competition. In this way, almost anything consumers would spend money on can be considered part of Coke's competitive set.

Different Competitive Frames

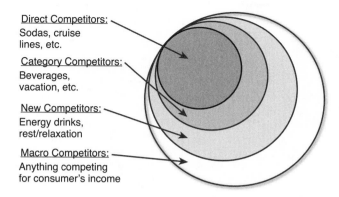

Direct Competitors:
Sodas, cruise
lines, etc.

Category Competitors:
Beverages,
vacation, etc.

New Competitors:
Energy drinks,
rest/relaxation

Macro Competitors:
Anything competing
for consumer's income

Figure 15.1 By understanding who your competitors are, you'll be better prepared to compete for consumers' disposable income.

Conducting a Social Media Competitive Assessment

Another way to take a look at your competitive set is to create a simple two-dimensional mapping scheme that can help you compare your brand's attributes against your competitor's attributes (see Figure 15.2). For our purposes, this two-dimensional mapping scheme can compare your brand's social media campaigns against your competitor's social media campaigns.

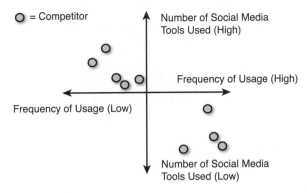

Figure 15.2 By plotting out how your competitors are using social media, you'll be able to analyze how to compete against them.

On one axis, you might consider the number of different social media tools that companies use. On the other axis, you might consider the frequency with which social media is used to communicate. Of course, an infinite number of possible dimensions can be used for competitive mapping. The goal is to select the dimensions that make the most sense in the context of your business, your industry, and your set of competitors. Often the most relevant are the ones that are most important to your target group of customers.

When you see where you are relative to your competition, you'll want to see how you can position yourself for success. Sure, many times a firm wants to place itself in exactly the same position as its closest competitor. Starbucks has MyStarbucksIdea.com, so Caribou Coffee has to develop the exact same type of tool and hope for the same resulting success. If it worked for Starbucks, why wouldn't it work for Caribou? This strategy has some merits.

Other times, you'll want to deliberately place yourself on the competitive grid as far away as possible from competitors. So if your nearest competitor has hired a specialist to manage its Facebook, Twitter, LinkedIn, and YouTube communications on a frequent basis, you might decide that you're interested in only a narrow set of tools—say, only blogs—and that you will contribute intermittently.

In reality, both of these approaches are at the extremes. To thwart competition, many clever companies deliberately segment, target, and position themselves to not directly compete. For example, when Southwest Airlines first came on the scene, management chose not to position the airline as just another airline. They were careful to consider the unique differentiators of Southwest's strategy—short flights, hub cities, relatively low prices, and hands-on service—to compare the Southwest travel experience to the alternative of driving, renting a car, taking a bus, or taking a train.

Similarly, when Walmart opened its first doors, it deliberately stayed away from the major metros where both Kmart and Sears dominated. Instead, it chose to locate its stores in rural areas and compete against smaller, independent retailers. When it dominated in that market, Walmart then had the muscle to penetrate urban locations and compete head to head against Kmart and Sears. The rest is history.

A final strategy that has worked well for some companies is to consider the concept of reverse positioning. Reverse positioning involves looking at what the major incumbents in your industry are doing, eliminating the obvious things that people offer in your business (sometimes doing the opposite), and adding several radically new points of difference.

As an example, Swedish furniture retailer IKEA uses reverse positioning. Most furniture stores provide high product quality, lots of product variety, lots of in-store assistance, and assembly and delivery. IKEA's positioning is average product quality, little variety within a category, little in-store assistance, and, until recently, no delivery and no assembly. How could they survive without the obvious "greens fees"? Instead of offering the obvious, they added a childcare center, a sit-down restaurant featuring Swedish favorites, unique accessories with cool names, and consistent, Scandinavian styling. The profit numbers show how successful this approach has been. Whereas most furniture stores either have closed or are on the verge of bankruptcy, IKEA's store revenues have steadily increased over the past three decades.

Some companies have found it better to zig while their competitors zag. This approach, called reverse positioning, has worked well for a variety of companies.

In the marketing communications space, smart marketers may want to replicate the IKEA success by including the competitive points of parity in terms of social media—must have a website, must have a Facebook page, must be using Twitter—and then think long and hard about what unique points of difference can successfully set the brand apart from the rest of its competitors. In terms of choice of social media tools, you want to analyze just how competition is using and benefiting from a specific tool and analyze whether it's worth the investment, given your marketing objectives.

A final point of comparison with marketing communications campaigns is their timing and intensity relative to competitive messages. Most traditional media have periods of "on" and "off" in terms of media scheduling. It's important for you to know when competitors have planned their communications and around what events as you plan for your own. With new media, particularly with pull-based social media, the conversation is ongoing. You have a lesser need to plan and time your actions based on your competition—and the same holds for them. So the only thing left is to make sure that your communications are consistent with your desired brand positioning and that your social media communications are integrated with the rest of your communications portfolio.

Let's take a look at the key concepts and action steps from this chapter:

- **Key concept**—You can analyze your competitive environment based on direct competitors, category competitors, new competitors, and macro competitors.

- **Action step**—Don't get myopic when thinking about your competition. In the broadest sense, every brand competes against every other brand for consumers' finite amount of disposable income.

- **Key concept**—By analyzing how your competitors are using social media, you can get a sense of what's working and what's not working within your industry.

- **Action step**—Analyze how your competitors are using social media to grow their business. Do a quick cost/benefit analysis to figure out what would work for your business and what wouldn't work.

- **Key concept**—Identifying how your competitors impact your business is critical to developing your unique positioning within the social media space.

- **Action step**—Try your hand at reverse positioning—remember IKEA versus all those now-defunct furniture companies—by monitoring the tools your competitors are using in the social media space. Either move away from them altogether or augment them with entirely unique tools or creative ways to use the tools.

16

Conducting an Internal Situation Analysis

Every good marketing plan starts with a situation analysis. It's the foundation upon which a company's marketing goals, objectives, strategies, and tactics are built.

When an organization develops a strategic plan of any kind, it must consider a number of things. It needs to consider the external environments in which it operates. It must fully understand the competitive landscape and where possible opportunity gaps exist. It has to develop a strong understanding of its customers and its prospects to create a value proposition that resonates well. Finally, it has to do an *internal situation analysis* to leverage strengths and downplay weaknesses.

This last factor, an internal situation analysis, is an important one. It's often overlooked because companies tend to shy away from doing a 360-degree analysis of their own strengths and weaknesses. Don't make that mistake. The only way you can know how to move forward with a successful social media campaign is to take a long, hard look at the "internal situation analysis mirror."

THE BIG IDEA

A situation analysis can help you analyze what's working and what's not working within your current marketing program. Before you move forward with your social media campaign, take a step back and do a situation analysis first.

Conducting an Internal Situation Analysis

In a typical marketing planning process, an internal organizational analysis looks at the relevant areas involving the product/service offering and the organization itself. In the same way, when you're thinking about social media planning, you need to review the successes and failures of past programs. In doing so, you will need to consider the fit between your desired social media strategy and the way your company is currently structured and operates.

You also need to look at the relative advantages and disadvantages of conducting social media activities in-house, as opposed to hiring an external agency or agencies. For example, the internal analysis may indicate that a firm is not capable of planning, implementing, and managing certain areas of the social media program. In this case, it might be wise to look for outside help in the form of a specialized agency.

Before you decide to hire an outside agency, you have to consider whether outsourcing a specific communications function will result in a loss of control or speed, and whether the resulting benefits of expertise and time will outweigh the negatives. For instance, both Calvin Klein and Macy's develop all their communications in-house. Macy's chooses to stay in-house because of the high frequency of communications and the need to stay on top of constant changes. Calvin Klein keeps communications in-house to retain complete control over the creative message and the brand's positioning.

In contrast, both Anheuser-Busch and Frito-Lay have traditionally chosen to work with large integrated marketing communications firms. Their belief is that specialized agencies will add more expertise to the communications process and will be able to develop creative marketing materials and content unique to each brand's position. After all, marketing communications firms are the experts when it comes to communications. Recently, however, Frito-Lay has deviated from its typical model of outsourcing to an agency by allowing user-generated advertising content for its Doritos brand. This may save Frito-Lay significant money, because the company doesn't have to pay for the agency's work, but it also risks altering the brand message because neither internal nor external "experts" are working on developing the brand communications.

Brand meaning develops over time. If the messages continuously get altered, so does strong brand meaning.

Conducting a SWOT Analysis

An internal situational analysis also assesses the relative strengths, weaknesses, opportunities, and threats (SWOT) of the product or service you're trying to sell. This information is particularly important to the creative personnel who must develop the communications message for the brand or company. Completing a SWOT analysis helps you identify ways to minimize the effect of weaknesses in your business while maximizing your strengths. Ideally, you'll match your strengths against market opportunities that result from your competitors' weaknesses or voids.

Here are some considerations when you do your social media SWOT analysis:

- **Strengths**—Think about what your company does well in terms of social media marketing. What makes you stand out from your competitors, and what they are doing? What advantages do you have over other businesses?

- **Weaknesses**—Identify what areas are a struggle from a management perspective. What resource limitations exist from a personnel perspective? What time constraints are present?

- **Opportunities**—Try to uncover areas where your strengths are not being fully utilized. Are there emerging trends that fit with your company's strengths? Are there new areas of social media growth that you should consider?

- **Threats**—Look both inside and outside your company for factors that could damage your business. Internally, do you have financial, development, or other problems? Externally, are your competitors becoming stronger through either their expertise or their messaging? Are emerging trends amplifying one of your weaknesses, or do you see other threats to your organization's success?

An internal situation analysis also involves assessing the strengths and weaknesses of the organization from an *image* perspective. The image an organization brings to the market has a significant impact on the way it can advertise and promote itself along with its various products and services. Companies or brands that are new to the market or those whose perceptions are negative may have to concentrate on their images, not just on the attributes and benefits of the products they sell. On the other hand, an organization with a strong reputation is already a step ahead when it comes to communication about its products or services.

For example, a recent nationwide survey found that companies with the best overall reputations among American consumers are Johnson & Johnson, The Coca-Cola Company, Hewlett-Packard, Intel, and Ben & Jerry's. When an organization's leaders understand what's at the core of their positive image, they can use it to grow their business. For example, Ben & Jerry's is regarded as a good citizen in its dealings with communities, employees, and the environment. The company capitalizes on this goodwill by supporting various community events and participating in programs that help the environment. That's good news for the nonprofits that benefit from Ben & Jerry's kindness, and it's good news for the Ben & Jerry's consumers, who know that a portion of each purchase goes to benefit those in need.

When an organization already has an established image, social media messages about the brand—either consistent or inconsistent with that image—can either add credibility or be downplayed if they are not accurate.

DID YOU KNOW?

The Ben & Jerry's Foundation donates almost $2 million each year to worthy causes around the U.S. This helps the nonprofits run their programs and also helps create a positive impression among Ben & Jerry's consumers.[1]

How to Move Ahead

For most organizations, developing a social media strategy involves some fundamental questions: How do the benefits of engaging in social media outweigh the risks? How can social media influence key organizational stakeholders in a way that benefits the organization? Does the organization have the capabilities needed to achieve its desired positioning by including social media in the communications mix?

Let's look at each of these questions in more detail. When people talk about benefits and risks, they usually think about the benefits and risks of engaging in a certain action. Often overlooked are the risks of *not* engaging in a certain action. For example, if your company is sitting on the social media sidelines, the inaction is creating a vacuum that's being filled by comments, blog posts, and tweets circulating on the Web that are not coming from you. In fact, these contributions can even be coming from competitors who want to tell a different story about you. That can be a dangerous situation.

So if it doesn't pay to sit on the sidelines, why do some companies do just that? According to a Marketing Sherpa survey of senior-level marketing managers, the most significant barrier to social media adoption named by 46 percent of respondents is "lack of knowledgeable staff." The problem is, a good percentage of those who consider themselves knowledgeable have limited social media experience. In fact, two-thirds of marketers at organizations that have not used social media marketing said they are "very" or "somewhat" knowledgeable about the subject. But without hands-on social media experience, this level of knowledge isn't very likely. It may be the reason "lack of knowledgeable staff" is seen as the most significant barrier.

What does all this mean? In a nutshell, it points out that, before you can move forward, it's best to take a step back. When you take a step back and conduct a situation analysis, you'll be able to get a clear picture of the strengths, weaknesses, opportunities, and threats facing your company. Only then will you be prepared to move forward to the next steps of looking at the consumer thought process, clarifying objectives, and developing key strategies designed to help you achieve those objectives.

Let's review these key concepts and action steps before moving on to the next chapter:

- **Key concept**—A critical component in developing your social media strategy and plan is understanding your organization's internal situation and determining whether you have the right structure, resources, and capabilities to manage social media in-house.

- **Action step**—Perform a SWOT analysis of your organization in terms of your ability to set up, run, and manage a social media campaign.

- **Key concept**—Some companies still fear moving ahead with their social media strategy development because they lack the knowledge of how to incorporate social media into their marketing communications plans.

- **Action step**—If you feel as though running a social media campaign in-house will take your eye off of running your business, hire an outside agency to develop it and run it for you.

Endnote

1. See BenAndJerrysFoundation.org.

17

Understanding the Customer Thought Process

The goal of marketing is to "get more people to buy more of your stuff, more often, for more money than they buy your competitor's stuff."

This phrase, describing the objectives for any marketer, comes from Sergio Zyman, the first chief marketing officer of The Coca-Cola Company. It sounds simple enough. In reality, doing all the activities in this short phrase requires disciplined strategy, focused operational detail, and a well-oiled organizational machine.

Most importantly, it requires a complete understanding of the needs of your customers so that you can "get more people to buy your stuff" over and over again. Often this is the hardest thing for an organization to do. It has to get inside the heads of its prospects and customers to understand what they truly want.

Having a strong understanding of what customers need involves being able to get an accurate picture of what they *think* they need. It also involves figuring out what they might need even if they don't tell you explicitly. That's the hard part.

To do this, you need to understand how customers make decisions and then understand how they respond to various stimuli, whether it's a traditional ad campaign or a social media campaign.

Customer Decision-Making Process

We've discussed a variety of consumer behavior models in previous chapters. They all point out that the decision-making process typically begins when a gap exists between the actual state people are in and their desired state (see Figure 17.1). This first stage, the problem recognition stage, occurs when a customer perceives a need and becomes motivated to solve the problem, as in, "I have a headache. I'd like to *not* have a headache."

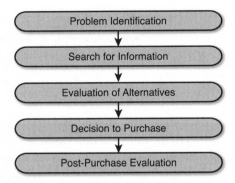

Figure 17.1 Consumers move through a series of states before, during, and after purchase.

For the most part, customers recognize that they have a need on their own. However, sometimes a marketer may be able to influence problem recognition by encouraging customers to be discontent with their current state or situation. For example, communications about personal hygiene products such as mouthwash, deodorant, and foot sprays may be designed to create insecurities that people can resolve by using these products.

The next stage in the process involves searching for information needed to make a purchase decision. Typically, this stage involves a prospect's memories about past experiences with the brand. If a search within a prospect's own memory or past experiences does not result in enough information, they'll seek additional information by searching for it in ads, on the Web, on television, or through some other medium. During this stage, a marketer can influence the decision through advertising, salespeople, point-of-purchase displays, and online tools. In the end, the goal is to get your brand into the customer's considered set of alternatives.

Once a prospect has gathered information about a brand, they start looking at alternatives. At this stage of the game, a marketer has an opportunity to create a positive brand impression or to change a negative attitude to a positive one.

The fourth stage in decision making is the actual purchase decision itself. After a customer has evaluated alternatives, that customer may develop a purchase intention or predisposition to buy a certain brand. However, a purchase decision is not the same as an actual purchase. The customer must still *make* the purchase. She still has to decide where to purchase, when to purchase, how much to spend, and so on. Considerable amounts of time can lapse between the *decision* to purchase and the *actual* purchase, particularly for high-involvement (such as high-dollar) purchases. As a result, almost half the time, a customer who has decided to purchase Brand A actually ends up buying Brand B.

DID YOU KNOW?

Research indicates that 47 percent of the time, a customer will report wanting to buy one product and end up buying a different product instead.[1]

Why is all this important? Because whether you're developing a social media campaign or a traditional marketing campaign, it's important to understand *how* and *why* people buy products. By studying consumer behavior, you can improve the effectiveness of your campaign and, in the long run, make more money.

Decision Making When It Really Matters

Let's consider a high-involvement decision: selecting which college to attend. This comes down to finding the right "fit." Students must determine which college lines up with their values, interests, and personality, and evaluate the university's academic programs, reputation, student life, cost, and other factors. In the end, prospective students must "feel right" about the college they choose.

Here's where social media comes in. How prospective students gather information to find that "good fit" has changed dramatically in the past 20 years. In those days, information and advice came from a narrow range of experts: school guidance counselors and whatever catalogs and directories happened to be on hand at the resource center. A few books on college admissions were written, but not many. No national rankings existed yet. Conversations with peers and perhaps other friends and family members were important, and noting where those others were going or had gone to college had an impact. But overall, the people who had an impact on this choice came from within a small, geographically defined circle.

THE BIG IDEA

Most decisions to buy a product happen after some experience or engagement with a brand. Social media can impact customers at various points in their decision-making process, thereby improving the ROI of your overall marketing campaign.

Since then, of course, the availability of information has grown tremendously in the form of direct marketing, glossy brochures, national rankings, published guidebooks, paid consultants and seminars, and even classes for high schoolers. Add to this the vast amounts of information available online from a variety of sources, including colleges themselves. Just the information to guide the "fit" decision is truly overwhelming, and sorting through it is as big a challenge as making the eventual decision.

Now add social media to the mix. The question is whether it will add value, by providing new kinds of information or by making it easier to sift through the most useful, relevant information from the marketplace of sources. One attribute that clearly distinguishes social media from other sources is that it makes peers more immediately and dynamically available. Prospective students are no longer limited to conversations with students at their own school or to the few students and alumni they encounter on a college tour or a campus event. They're not even limited by the representative peers quoted in a guidebook. Using social media, they can largely bypass college officials, consultants, and other "experts"—not to mention parents—and connect with peers from the national and even global landscape.

How will these connections made possible by social media, in conjunction with traditional media, influence the decisions of prospects and the admissions and marketing strategies of colleges and universities? Will the marketing efforts of colleges and all those "adult" voices and experts become less influential now that prospects can access the "authentic voice," or at least voices that feel authentic because they come from peers?

Prospective students find social media conversations attractive and useful because the voices are authentic and impartial. Information has already been democratized; schools such as MIT that present student blogs on their admissions websites are acknowledging the situation— and perhaps trying to create a competitive advantage by bringing some of those conversations "in-house." As the volume of choice and information grows, consumers turn to the sources they feel they can trust.

DID YOU KNOW?

Seventy percent of the respondents to a survey by Nielsen "completely" trusted or "somewhat" trusted recommendations from consumer opinions posted online. That was second only to "recommendations from people known," which came in at 90 percent.[2]

The customer decision process doesn't end with a purchase. After using the product or service, a customer compares the level of performance with expectations and is either satisfied or dissatisfied. Positive performance means that the brand stays in a customer's evoked set of brands, and there's a strong likelihood that the customer will choose the brand chosen again. A negative performance may lead the customer to form negative attitudes toward the brand, decreasing the likelihood that the customer will purchase the brand again, or even causing it to drop out of the customer's evoked set.

The Role of Social Media in Influencing Decisions

So how does social media tie into the customer's decision-making process? At first glance, it may seem that the main purpose of social media is to drive awareness and to perhaps impact the problem recognition stage. After all, more people are having conversations about a company, a product, or a brand before the actual purchase. However, the real value of social media might lie in the consideration stage, or the alternative evaluation stage, in terms of establishing relevance. Customers are more likely to consider a product or service that their friends or other people like them have recommended than they are to consider one recommended by outside sources that they don't know. Social media therefore helps customers reduce their choice by narrowing the list to a smaller set of possible alternatives.

Moreover, marketers must recognize the importance of the post-purchase evaluation stage of decision making. Dissatisfied customers who experience post-purchase doubt or have had a negative experience not only are unlikely to rebuy, but also may spread negative word-of-mouth information that deters others from purchasing a particular product or service. In this way, blogs, consumer ratings, and product reviews can directly impact future customer decision making and choice.

In addition to understanding the complexities of customer decision making, you'll want to understand consumer response to communications. Consumer response refers to the various steps or processes that those who receive communications may go through in moving toward a specific behavior (such as purchasing a product) and how the promotional efforts of a marketer influence consumer response.

Many models of consumer response have been developed, but one of the most relevant models to the inclusion of social media in the communications mix is the AIDA model (see Figure 17.2). We mentioned AIDA in Chapter 4, "How to Speak Social Media," but let's briefly recap what it's all about. AIDA stands for Awareness, Interest, Desire, and Action. The model was first developed to represent the stages through which a salesperson must take a customer in the personal selling process. First, a marketing campaign (or salesperson) needs to get the customer's *attention*. Then it needs to arouse some *interest* in the product or service. Strong levels of interest should create a *desire* to own or use the product.

Finally, the *action* stage involves getting the customer to make a purchase commitment and closing the sale.

Consumer Behavior Models				
	AIDA Model	Hierarchy of Effects Model	Innovation Adoption Model	Information Processing Model
Cognition Phase	Attention	Awareness, Knowledge	Awareness	Presentation, Attention, Comprehension
Affective Phase	Interest, Desire	Liking, Preference, Conviction	Interest, Evaluation	Yielding, Retention
Behavioral Phase	Action	Purchase	Adoption	Behavior

Figure 17.2   A variety of different consumer behavior models exist, but they all point to the same goal: converting a prospect to a customer.

Different forms of communication have been shown to have varying effects on the response stages. Advertising is largely effective in driving awareness. Direct mail and websites are strong drivers of interest. Personal selling and PR are often responsible for driving desire, and sales promotion often leads to action by encouraging trial. The impact of these different media types varies depending on the level of involvement a customer has with the product category and based on the degree of differentiation between alternatives.

As with traditional media, social media can be segmented to reflect what consumer response it can best achieve. Twitter, Facebook, Google+, and Instagram are the strongest tools for driving awareness as well as desire. LinkedIn and Pinterest might be best for driving interest. In terms of action, e-mail marketing may be the strongest driver. Still left to be determined is exactly what messages work best on each platform. The best way to answer that is to run your own A/B split tests and to track your results.

With all this in mind, let's take a spin through the key concepts and action steps from this chapter:

- **Key concept**—Customers follow a consistent process when they are making decisions. Marketers can influence the sequence of these stages and how long a customer takes in each of these decision stages.

- **Action step**—Map out the decision-making process for different segments of customers, and understand where and how you can influence this decision making with a variety of social media tools.

- **Key concept**—Customers follow specific patterns of response based on their exposure to marketing stimuli, their level of involvement in the product, and the degree of differentiation they perceive among competing alternatives.

- **Action step**—Understand the level of involvement your customer has with your product or brand, and determine how differentiated you are from your competitors. These two factors will impact the actual response pattern customers follow and will help you determine which social media stimuli to use.

Endnotes

1. J. Scott Armstrong, Vicki G. Morwitz, and V. Kumar, "Sales Forecasts for Existing Consumer Products and Services: Do Purchase Intentions Contribute to Accuracy?" *International Journal of Forecasting* 16 (2000): 383–397.

2. http://blog.nielsen.com/nielsenwire/consumer/ global-advertising-consumers-trust-real-friends-and- virtual-strangers-the-most/

18

Establishing Your Major Objectives and Key Strategies

The Detroit Zoo had been a tourist destination for more than 80 years, but it now had a problem. Unbeknownst to most visitors, it faced financial hardship caused by circumstances that had begun a few years earlier.

The city of Detroit, which provided a significant portion of the zoo's operating budget, cut all of its financial support of zoo operations a few years earlier. As the new summer season approached, reality set in: In a matter of months, the money would run out. The zoo was faced with the very real possibility of closing its doors.

Only one option was left. The zoo had to appeal directly to taxpayers. A new tax was proposed to provide the necessary funding to keep the zoo afloat. Zoo management had to convince voters to pass the requested new tax, or the zoo would close. With the very real possibility that there would no longer be a Detroit Zoo and the impact that would have on the children of Detroit, zoo officials had just one objective for an integrated marketing campaign they were planning to launch: Get residents to vote "yes" on a new ten-year property tax to support the zoo.

Zoo management could have simply created an awareness campaign highlighting all the great attractions at the zoo. Or it could have created a promotional campaign appealing to visitors by offering some sort of discount or incentive. Instead, it chose to stay focused on the main issue at hand: raising money to keep the zoo afloat. By taking a step back and thinking through the situation before taking a step forward, they were able to identify three important factors leading to a successful campaign: the key drivers, the primary objectives, and the desired outcomes.

Don't Just Create an Action—Create a Chain Reaction

Zoo management knew that it needed a message that would provoke not just action, but a chain reaction. They distilled the big idea into a single concept: *Our Zoo Is Worth Keeping*. They also made it personal—"The Detroit Zoo Is *Our* Zoo"—and highly emotional, drawing attention to the interaction children have with the animals at the zoo. By tapping into these key emotional drivers, they were able to set themselves up for success.

Advertising led this initiative, but it involved more than just a traditional advertising message. It relied on a powerful dialogue that used mass media and new media to create a conversation in the news and on the streets. A public relations and grassroots effort to get the "Worth Keeping" message to both residents and influencers kept the conversation front and center in the news for about a month leading up to the election.

When the vote was finally taken, zoo officials were pleased to find that voters had approved the new tax with larger margins than anyone had imagined. Having achieved this, zoo management was in a position to implement some of the strategies required to get people not only to see the zoo in a new light, but also to become reengaged with the zoo in terms of attendance, volunteering, and finances.

How to Set Objectives That Get You Results

The main point of the Detroit Zoo example is that results such as these are attainable only when you 1) identify the *key drivers* for success, 2) develop specific *campaign objectives,* and 3) know exactly which *outcomes* you are seeking to achieve. The trick is to think through all this first, before you start to develop your approach or your strategy to achieve them.

Setting objectives and developing strategy takes discipline. It takes forming a unified view of the problem, making an assessment about desired outcomes, and having a shared vision within your organization on how to achieve those outcomes.

If you're thinking that your organization has had trouble articulating just what you hope to achieve by using social media, you're not alone. Unfortunately, many organizations have difficulty when it comes to setting realistic objectives for a social media program.

THE BIG IDEA

When setting social media objectives, it's important to be SMART. In other words, you need to set objectives that are specific, measurable, attainable, realistic, and time bound. Only then can you determine the best strategy to take and the best customers to target.

Numerous articles and blog posts talk about how to set objectives for a social media campaign. The objectives mentioned range from driving website traffic to increasing customer engagement. But no matter what your stated objectives are, only one thing is important: You need to integrate your social media campaign into your marketing campaign so that they can both show a quantifiable return on your investment.

Moving Product

To many managers, the only meaningful objective for their promotional strategies is sales. They take the position that the basic reason to spend money on any kind of communications, including communications via social media, is to sell a product or service. This makes a lot of sense. Ultimately, the goal of any marketing program is to sell more products or services, resulting in more revenue, higher market share, and more profit.

Not long ago, two of the three largest oral care manufacturers, Unilever and Colgate–Palmolive, joined Procter & Gamble in marketing at-home tooth-whitening kits. In their product launches, Unilever spent about $20 million on Mentadent and Colgate allocated $60 million to Simply White. Colgate's objective was to get an immediate $100 million in sales in the first year (a third of the total market); Mentadent focused on in-store efforts, sales promotions, ads in beauty magazines and on the company's websites, and professional outreach programs to gain its share of the market.

Sales-oriented objectives such as the ones Unilever and Colgate–Palmolive set for themselves can make a great deal of sense. But focusing only on sales objectives has its challenges. In the real world, poor sales can result from a number of uncontrollable factors, including product design, quality, packaging, distribution, pricing, demographic trends, and competitor actions. Furthermore, social media can make people aware of a brand, but it can't make them buy it—particularly if something else is fundamentally wrong. For example, in the early 1990s, when Nabisco launched Snackwell's, a line of reduced-fat and nonfat cookies, the advertising for Snackwell's is what drove consumers to the stores. The advertising was brilliant, but the factories couldn't meet the rate of the demand and the store shelves were always short of packages.

Another problem when considering only sales-oriented objectives for social media is that the effects of advertising often occur over an extended period of time. Your social media marketing efforts can have a lag or a carryover effect. In other words, the money and time that you spend on social media efforts don't necessarily have an immediate impact on sales. That doesn't mean you should abandon your efforts. If you're trying to grow your sales, you need to consider that the impact of social media may emerge over time and that, besides sales, social media may help you achieve other important milestones that lead to revenue growth.

DID YOU KNOW?

Mobile phones are an increasingly important way to connect with your customers. In fact, a study by the 60 Second Marketer found that more people around the globe own a mobile phone than own a toothbrush.[1]

How to Move People

As we described in early sections of the book, marketing communications can have a cumulative effect over time and can result in various intermediate stages of persuasion that eventually lead to sales. Advertising and other forms of promotion, including all forms of social media, are designed to achieve communications such as brand knowledge and interest, favorable attitudes and image, and purchase intentions or leads. With some types of communication, you can't expect a direct sales response immediately. Instead, marketers realize that they have to provide relevant information and create favorable predispositions toward a brand before customers purchase anything.

The Communications Effect Pyramid (see Figure 18.1) depicts the way social media helps move people—or trigger some kind of presales response. At the lower level of the pyramid, your brand's communications first get people to pay attention to and become knowledgeable about the product or service. At the next level, the goal is to get people to develop an interest, a liking, and perhaps even a preference for your product or service. Beyond knowledge, you want people to develop feelings. Finally, at the top of the pyramid comes action. At this top level, people develop strong convictions, form purchase intentions, and finally purchase.

Communications Effect Pyramid

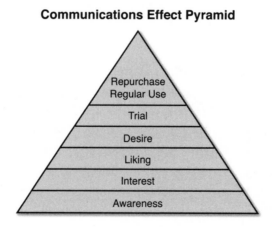

Figure 18.1 Understanding the consumer response process is one step involved in setting objectives for your campaign.

Part of driving communications objectives involves encouraging prospective customers to start dialogues with you and with each other about

---

your products and services. You want to get them engaged so that, over time, you can convert them to customers. If you do this correctly, existing customers will not only repurchase from you, but they will become strong advocates for your brand and help you continue the dialogue within and outside your brand community.

Whether you decide to focus on using your social media to drive immediate sales or future sales often depends on where you sit in an organization. If you're in the CEO or CFO office, you may be interested in driving immediate sales so that this quarter's numbers look good to Wall Street. But if you're in the CMO office or on the agency side, you might believe that building long-term demand is just as important as generating short-term sales blips.

In the end, the path you choose might boil down to whether you consider your social marketing efforts to be an investment that will show returns at some point in the future or whether you consider your social marketing efforts to be an investment that you must quickly recoup. To know how to balance these two major objectives of moving product and moving people, you might have to think about who is sitting in the CEO seat of your organization and understand what drives that person's business strategy.

Developing Your Social Media Strategy

After you've outlined your specific social media objectives, you're ready to develop a social media strategy. Your social media strategy is a subset of your overall marketing strategy. And your marketing strategy is a subset of your business strategy.

Keep all these factors in mind as you move forward with a social media campaign. After all, one-off marketing campaigns that create short-term blips don't grow a business in the long run. Only well-thought-out campaigns with an eye toward strategy and execution succeed.

A successful social media campaign isn't something to merely play around with in between meetings or to give to an intern as a task to complete over the summer. It should be an intentional, thought-provoking extension of your organization that helps you drive your business objectives.

Companies often ask themselves these questions when developing an overall business strategy:

- Should we be first to market and enjoy first-mover advantages, or should we pursue a wait-and-follow approach?

- Should we try to enter with a low-cost position, or should we try to distinguish ourselves from competitors with a differentiated offering?

- Should we approach the market as a whole, or should we focus on a single or a few niche segments?

- Should we grow our business by encouraging more sales of our existing product to our existing customers, by introducing new products, by entering new markets, or all three?

Take a look at these questions and develop answers for your own company. Then take a step back and analyze whether the social media strategy you're developing fits within the business strategy you've outlined from similar questions. You'll then have taken the first steps toward developing a methodical, strategic approach to a successful social media campaign.

We've covered a lot of ground again. Let's take a quick look at the key concepts from this chapter and their action steps:

- **Key concept**—When developing any marketing campaign, you need to 1) identify the *key drivers* for success, 2) develop specific *campaign objectives*, and 3) know exactly which *outcomes* you are seeking to achieve.

- **Action step**—Get all members of your marketing team in a room together (along with other interested parties) and map out key drivers, campaign objectives, and outcomes for your social media campaign.

- **Key concept**—Social media objectives can be categorized into two major buckets. The first objective is to move product to drive *immediate* sales. The second objective is to move people (that is, drive awareness, interest, and desire) to drive *future* sales.

- **Action step**—Find out what your organization expects in terms of return on investment and the time frame for that return. You can then determine whether your social media campaign needs to drive immediate sales or future sales. Remember, they're not mutually exclusive—if you have a big budget, you can accomplish both.

- **Key concept**—When using social media, it's critical for your campaign to tie to your business objectives and for these business objectives to link to your overall business strategy.

- **Action step**—Make sure you clearly understand your organization's business objectives and the strategy it's using to accomplish those objectives. Ask key players within your organization to define the business objectives and strategy or to direct you to the appropriate documentation.

Endnote

1. http://60secondmarketer.com/blog/2011/10/18/
   more-mobile-phones-than-toothbrushes/

19

Aligning Your Social Media Strategy with Your Brand Essence

One of the biggest mistakes people make when setting up a social media campaign is to not align their social media campaign with their primary marketing campaign. As a result, they talk to consumers with two different voices, which is never a good idea.

In this chapter, we talk about aligning your social media campaign with your brand. What is a brand? A brand is often defined as the sum total of consumers' perceptions and feelings about the product attributes, how it performs, and the benefits it provides to the consumers. Said another way, a brand develops from the spoken and unspoken messages a consumer receives about your product or service.

Brands are created through a wide range of touchpoints. Every time a customer interacts with your brand, the customer forms associations. In this way, a brand is much like the promise of a specific customer experience.

THE BIG IDEA

Articulating your brand essence through your social media strategy is the key to successful marketing. Whatever you want your brand to represent should be articulated and demonstrated in your social media communication efforts.

The most successful brands have established a relevant, differentiated meaning for themselves and have reduced this meaningful difference to a simple, clear, and cohesive thought. This clear and concise articulation of what a brand stands for is known as *brand essence*.

Does all that make sense? Sometimes brand theory and brand strategy can get a little over the top, but the bottom line is that a brand is the sum total of the experiences and perceptions a prospect or customer has about your product or service.

The Essence of Brand Essence

Think of brand essence as the heart and soul of a product or service. It represents the relationship your brand has with your customer. For example, Hallmark uses the phrase, "Enriching Lives" to capture its brand essence and its company culture. "Enriching Lives" represents the basis for how Hallmark serves customers, develops its products, communicates its marketing messages, develops merchandising for its stores, and creates a positive work environment for employees. Hallmark's brand essence permeates every aspect of the company and business, and it has continued to serve the brand over time.

Similarly, Harley-Davidson's brand essence has created a fiercely loyal customer base that connects to the brand emotionally. Harley-Davidson's image doesn't simply reflect the quality and design of its motorcycles. Rather, the brand is best known for the value it places on nonconformity and self-determination. That's why buyers believe that owning a Harley makes a powerful, strong statement to others that they live life on their own terms.

DID YOU KNOW?

If you want to get a basic understanding of your brand essence, you can do three simple things:

1. Conduct external focus groups or surveys with customers and prospects to uncover their impressions of your brand.

2. Conduct internal focus groups or surveys with your employees to uncover their impressions of your brand.

---

3. Compare and contrast your findings to begin to understand the current essence of your brand.

Getting a deep understanding of your brand essence is often much more complicated than what we've outlined here, but if you want a basic understanding, you can follow these three simple steps.

Before you begin thinking about how to align your social media efforts with your brand, you must first articulate exactly what your brand stands for or means. You also need to know how your prospects, customers, and employees interpret that meaning. For example, when you think about the brand Volvo, the word *safety* immediately comes to mind. In contrast, when you think about the brand Rolls-Royce, *luxury* comes to mind. Of course, there are elements of safety within the Rolls-Royce brand and elements of luxury in some models of Volvo, but the primary promise of each of these brands forms its unique essence.

It may sound simple to articulate your brand's meaning or essence, but this can be a challenging endeavor. Several gaps may exist. First, there could be gap between your existing brand articulation and what you would like your brand to represent. For example, Mercedes may want to retain its positioning as a luxury brand, but that's not the current perception people have of the brand as it has rolled out several lower-priced line extensions during the last decade or so. Another gap may be between your intended brand positioning and the actions you take to communicate that positioning. Going back to the Mercedes example, Mercedes may want to exemplify luxury, but rolling out a line of cars priced under $30,000, a line of bicycles, and even a line of children's tricycles goes against a luxury positioning. That's a disconnect from the consumer's point of view.

Aligning Your Efforts with Your Brand

When you have a good handle on your brand's essence, you need to think about how to communicate that essence through traditional and new media. This is where social media comes in. With the right content on your blog posts, tweets, and Facebook fan pages, you have the potential to spread your brand messages quickly across a wide range of audiences. However, you must ensure that the content you develop is consistent with the image you want to portray. Putting out quality and focused content helps you establish your brand only if your content supports your brand's essence and positioning.

The goal of social media is to help you develop personal relationships between your brand and your target audience. The interactive aspect of social media is personal by nature, so the relationships you create can be *deeper and longer lasting* than with any other media. To maintain those relationships, make sure your brand comes across as being authentic, and your promises must be transparent.

One of the keys is to be consistent in what you say and do in your social media campaign in order to ensure proper alignment between your actions and your brand's promise.

Let's take a look at an example of a misaligned social media campaign and then consider an example of a well-aligned social media campaign, to put what we've articulated into context.

The Good, the Bad, and the Ugly

When Honda decided to publish its Crosstour's photos on Facebook, it should have been ready for some serious feedback. Within a short time, its fan page was flooded with negative comments regarding the look of Honda's new Cross Utility Vehicle. Most "fans" clearly were not too thrilled with the new design. But soon afterward, they saw some positive comments about the model. The problem was, the positive comments were coming from Honda's product manager, who didn't disclose his own relationship with the company until the angry fans called him out. This likely made people think twice about Honda's ability to be true to its brand essence.

DID YOU KNOW?

A negative remark on social media equates to a loss of 30 potential customers—but this also means that a positive review may help you gain 30 new customers.[1]

Of course, companies need to use social media to promote their products, but if they get bad feedback, they shouldn't try to manipulate it. Social media users are savvy enough to expose you if they want to. Honesty and authenticity are critical to success in this space.

In contrast to the Honda example, let's take a look at a company that seems to have done everything right to align its social media strategy with its brand and what it stands for. Everyone talks about using social media to connect with customers and engage in deeper relationships and conversations, but few companies are able to do it well. One company that seems to be doing this right is Starbucks.

The Starbucks strategy involves several elements, including a presence on Facebook, Twitter, YouTube, and Flickr. As mentioned previously, one of the company's key social media tactics has been to develop the MyStarbucksIdea.com website. My Starbucks Idea opens the concept of crowdsourcing to any customer willing to register. But the "Starbucks Ideas In Action" blog, at the website, acts as a counterpart to the My Starbucks Idea content. The blog is written by different Starbucks employees and talks about how they implemented an idea or are reacting to the suggestions and information from customers. An interesting aspect of this blog is that readers can provide feedback and comments. Many corporate blogs don't allow that. But by being open to a second level of feedback, Starbucks can continue the dialogue with customers and extend the Starbucks experience *outside* the store.

DID YOU KNOW?

You can reuse your content across multiple platforms as long as you don't duplicate it 100 percent across different sites. If you duplicate the content exactly, search engines might think you're trying to spam the system. However, repurposed content that borrows from your original content is fine.

Social media is a relatively new medium, but its newness does not preempt the traditional rules of marketing. Whether you're attempting to "sell" yourself as an industry expert or build buzz and kick-start sales of a breakthrough product your company has just developed, you must determine who your likely buyers are, whether they hang out on the social media circuit, and how to generate content that appeals to them.

Embarking on a social media campaign is time consuming and, therefore, expensive. Although hitting the Tweet button has virtually no cost, a social media campaign must be planned, nurtured, tracked, and managed with the same vigilance of any other marketing campaign. Social media often allows for an intimate look at your brand, so letting the summer intern run amuck posting on behalf of your organization is probably not the best strategy.

Let's take a quick look at our key concepts and action steps before we move on to the next chapter:

- **Key concept**—It's critical to have a well-defined brand before you embark on a social media marketing campaign.

- **Action step**—Perform an audit of your brand to determine whether gaps exist in one of the following places: 1) between what you *are* and what you want to *be,* 2) between what you want to be and how your customers perceive you, and 3) between what you want to be and what you can be based on your organizational resources, structure, and strategy.

- **Key concept**—Your social media strategy must align with your brand's essence for your marketing efforts to work together.

- **Action step**—Identify key drivers of brand essence and use them to develop your marketing communications strategy. Your social media strategy should also be developed based on this same set of key drivers, to achieve maximum communications impact.

- **Key concept**—Brands that are transparent and authentic have a better chance of success with consumers than brands that aren't.

- **Action step**—Be authentic and transparent 100 percent of the time. No exceptions.

Endnote

1. www.penn-olson.com/2010/04/20/4-disturbing-social-media-statistics-for-businesses/

20

How to Measure the Impact of Your Social Media Campaign

When you think about it, the only truly important social media metric is good old return on investment (ROI). Everything else—traffic, comments, followers, leads—is just a stop along the way.

Without a positive ROI, there's really no reason to run a social media campaign (unless you're doing it just for kicks). If your social media campaign doesn't have a positive ROI, it won't be long before you get a knock on the door from the CFO or CEO telling you to shut the whole thing down.

It's a good idea to keep ROI on your radar screen at all times. It's easy to get distracted by the minutiae of running a campaign, but ROI should be front and center in everything you do.

One of the ways we keep ROI in our sights is by using something we've come up with called the social media management principle (see Figure 20.1). This simple concept divides social media content into things that are *distractions* and things that are *attractions*.

A social media distraction takes you away from the task of generating a positive ROI for your company. Common distractions are articles, videos, and other content that fall into several categories: fun and games, friends and family, sports and hobbies, and other unrelated activities. It's fine to spend time on those kinds of things after hours, but during work, it's best to keep them to a minimum.

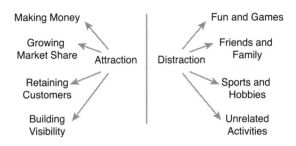

Social Media Management Principle

Making Money

Growing Market Share — Attraction

Retaining Customers

Building Visibility

Fun and Games

Distraction — Friends and Family

Sports and Hobbies

Unrelated Activities

Figure 20.1 Using the social media management principle keeps you focused on the most important task: making money.

On the other hand are social media *attractions,* which can help you improve your social media ROI. They include articles, videos, and other content that help you make money, grow market share, retain customers, or build visibility.

Keep the social media management principle in mind as you run your campaign. It's easy to get distracted when you're running a social media campaign, so be sure to focus on what will help you generate a positive ROI.

Setting Objectives for Your Campaign

Shortly, we'll talk about how to *measure* a social media campaign, but first let's cover *setting objectives.* After all, there's no point in measuring anything unless you have a clear set of business objectives in mind.

We've established that the ultimate objective for most social media campaigns is a positive ROI. A positive ROI is the result of converting a prospect to a customer. In Chapter 23, "All Roads in Social Media Should Lead to ROI," we talk about these objectives in greater detail, but for now, keep these points in mind:

- *The objective for some social media campaigns is to drive* **immediate** *sales.* As mentioned previously, Dell Computers uses this model with its DellOutlets Twitter page. The tweets on the

DellOutlets page are specifically designed to drive immediate sales.

- *The objective for other social media campaigns is to drive* **future sales.** The MyStarbucksIdea.com website is designed to create Awareness, Interest, Desire, and Action (AIDA). You can't buy a cup of coffee on the MyStarbucksIdea.com website—but you sure can build up a desire for one there.

- *The objective for still other social media campaigns is to reduce churn.* The Discover Card customer relationship management campaign discussed in the first chapter is designed to reduce churn and increase loyalty. In effect, that increases ROI, even though it doesn't result in a direct sale.

Keep each of these points in mind as you're thinking about your own social media campaign. Be sure to ask yourself, "Do I want do drive sales immediately? Or do I want to build demand for future sales? Or do I want to reduce churn and increase loyalty?" They're all important objectives, and they're not mutually exclusive.

The Seven Deadly Sins of Social Media Measurement

The seven deadly sins of social media measurement are the most common mistakes people make in measuring social media. It's a good idea to be aware of these as you move forward. After all, it's sometimes easier to learn from others' mistakes than to learn from their successes:

- **Deadly Sin #1: Not measuring your social media campaign—** Not measuring anything around your social media campaign is, well, not very smart. Surprisingly, many people dive into social media without setting up a plan for measurement. Remember, you need to set your business objectives first and then determine how you're going to measure against those objectives. We think of this as taking a step back before you take a step forward. It's a good approach.

- **Deadly Sin #2: Measuring everything**—Social media is primarily digital in nature, so just about anything can be tracked. You can keep an eye on uploads, downloads, ratings, comments, bookmarks, fans, followers, and a slew of other things. But if you don't have a plan behind what you're measuring, you'll end up with too much data. Believe it or not, you can run a successful social media campaign by keeping track of as few as five to ten key metrics.

- **Deadly Sin #3: Measuring the wrong thing**—It's easy to get distracted with social media. Many people go on tangents and measure things that don't lead to *making money*. Remember, in our opinion, the only reason to run a social media campaign is to eventually make money (or reduce costs), so be sure everything you do points in that direction.

- **Deadly Sin #4: Measuring just to measure**—Don't just measure something because you can. After all, there's no point in having information if you don't also have *insight*. Spend some time developing insights using the data you do have. For example, don't just track the data that shows the average person visits only 1.5 pages on your site. Try to understand *why* people visit only 1.5 pages, and then try to get them to increase their page views to 2.0 per visit and more.

- **Deadly Sin #5: Not tracking your progress**—If you're taking the time and trouble to measure something, be sure you can compare it to past performance. That way, when you see improvement over time, you can go into the CEO and say, "See? I told you this social media stuff works. Here's proof, Mr. Big Shot." (*Please be advised:* Don't call your CEO "Mr. Big Shot" unless you're on very good terms with him.)

- **Deadly Sin #6: Not sharing your progress**—Remember the CEO you were calling Mr. Big Shot? Whether or not you call your CEO that, be sure to share your results with all the relevant members of your management team. It's better to over-share than to not share enough. You always want key influencers and decision makers within your company to be aware of your social media successes.

- **Deadly Sin #7: There is no seventh deadly sin**—There are only six deadly sins of social media measurement. But if we called this section "The Six Deadly Sins of Social Media Measurement," it wouldn't have the same ring to it, so we called it "The Seven Deadly Sins of Social Media Measurement." Can you think of a seventh deadly sin of social media measurement? If so, let us know about it. Just visit 60SecondMarketer.com/SeventhDeadly-Sin and add yours to the growing list of social media deadly sins.

Those are the seven—okay, *six*—deadly sins of social media measurement. Keep them in mind as you set the foundation for your social media measurement program.

Segmenting Social Media Measurement into Categories

This list includes just some of the things you can measure in a social media campaign. After a while, it gets pretty confusing—and if you tried measuring everything on the list, you'd end up with a lot of *information* but little *insight*. Because of that, we are going to categorize the information into three groups—but first, let's look at a list of *some* of the things you can measure:

- Twitter followers
- Facebook fans
- Comments
- Social bookmarks
- Page views
- Inbound links
- Click-throughs
- Leads generated
- Ratings
- Downloads
- Conversions

- CPM
- Likes/Favorites
- Uploads
- Growth rate of fans, followers, and friends
- Online mentions across blogs, microblogs, message boards, and so on
- Geographic distribution of mentions
- Positive and negative sentiment surrounding your brand
- Viral video activity
- Bounce rate

These are just some of the hundreds of things you can measure in a social media campaign, and you can see by this short list that it can get pretty confusing pretty quickly.

QUICK START GUIDE

Let's break things down into three easy steps so you know how to move forward:

1. *Measure the quantity.* These social media metrics are quantitative in nature. By that, we mean that the metrics simply measure data and have little emotional content. They include the number of Twitter followers, the number of inbound links, the geographic distribution of mentions, the click-through rates, and other items that are data-centric in nature.

2. *Measure the quality.* These social media metrics are qualitative in nature. They provide information about the emotions, thoughts, and intensity of feelings about your product or service. (For example, if people use "cheap" to describe your product, it's not the same thing as if they say "inexpensive.")

> 3. *Measure the ROI.* These social media metrics help you track your progress toward your ultimate goal, which is to make money with social media. They include metrics such as leads generated, customers retained, prospects converted, and, most important, profits generated.

In upcoming chapters, we dive deeper into these categories of social media measurement tools. For now, let's do a recap of the key concepts and action steps from this chapter:

- **Key concept**—The most important social media metric is your return on investment (ROI).

- **Action step**—It's easy to get distracted by other important metrics, but every other metric you measure should ultimately lead to ROI. Always keep your social media ROI on your radar screen.

- **Key concept**—The social media management principle is a way to stay focused on social media tools that help you make money, grow market share, retain customers, or build visibility.

- **Action step**—Sketch out the social media management principle on a yellow sticky note and attach it to your computer monitor. Seriously, try it. It sounds silly, but it'll keep you focused on the only thing that's important: generating a positive ROI.

- **Key concept**—Social media campaigns come in several flavors: those that help you generate immediate sales; those that help you generate future sales; those that help you reduce churn or increase brand loyalty.

- **Action step**—Figure out which of the three kinds of social media campaigns you want. Remember, they're not mutually exclusive, so you can have all three.

- **Key concept**—The deadly sins of social media measurement are the most common mistakes people make when measuring their social media campaigns.

- **Action step**—Review all six deadly sins of social media measurement and make a recommendation for a seventh deadly sin at 60SecondMarketer.com/SeventhDeadlySin.

- **Key concept**—Social media measurement involves following a process. Step 1 measures the quantity. Step 2 measures the quality. Step 3 measures the ROI.

- **Action step**—Keep these three categories in mind as you develop your social media campaign. By grouping your social media measurement tools into these categories, you'll be able to stay more organized in your approach.

21

Measuring the Quantitative Data

In the previous chapter, we mentioned that it's easier to wrap your mind around all the ways you can measure social media if you lay it out in three distinct steps. Step 1 is measuring the quantity. Step 2 is measuring the quality. Step 3 is measuring the return on investment (ROI).

Measuring the *quantity* gives you insight into the volume of traffic your social media campaign is generating. A basic metric for measuring quantity is the number of Twitter followers or Facebook fans you have. That's pretty straightforward.

Measuring the *quality* gives you insight into the emotions, thoughts, and feelings surrounding your brand. By studying the emotional component of your social media campaign, you'll be able to get a sense of how loyal people are to your brand and what inner needs are being fulfilled by your brand's social media campaign.

Measuring the *ROI* is, of course, the most important metric. By analyzing your leads generated, prospects converted, customers retained, and profits generated, you'll be able to track your progress on your ultimate goal, which is to make money with social media.

Measuring Traffic on Your Own Website

We're going to kick off this chapter by talking about step 1, the *quantitative* measurement of your campaign. Quantitative measurements give you an understanding of how people are engaging with your brand online.

The first and easiest way to get a quantitative measurement of your social media program is to track data using some popular and readily-available tools. These tools provide in-depth information that let you track data such as number of visits, page views, pages per visit, bounce rate, reach, and average time on site.

DID YOU KNOW?

Your **bounce rate** is the percentage of visitors who only visited one page on your site. So, if your web-site bounce rate is 81%, it means that 81% of the people visiting your site either hit the back button on their browser or closed out the tab after visiting just one page on your site. Your **exit rate** is the percentage of page views to a particular page that were the last in the session. As an example, if your About Us page has a 75% exit rate, it means that 75% of the people who visited your About Us page exited the site after viewing that page.[1]

Here's a quick rundown of these important tools:

- **Google Analytics**—What's not to like about Google Analytics? By dropping a line of code into your website, you can track how people get to your site, how they navigate through your site, and how long they stay on your site. Google Analytics is getting more and more cumbersome, which can get in the way of using it sometimes, but overall it's really a brilliant tool that everyone with a website should be using.

- **KISSmetrics**—These guys try to be what Google Analytics is not. In other words, they take data and try to help you make sense out of it instead of just dumping it into your lap. Each piece of data is tied to a real person so that you can get a sense of where they are in your sales funnel. KISSmetrics was founded by Neil Patel who runs a well-respected blog called QuickSprout (not to be confused with SproutSocial, discussed next).

- **SproutSocial**—With SproutSocial, you can publish posts to your social media channels while at the same time monitoring how people are responding to those posts. They have an easy-to-use dashboard that provides just the right amount of data and information so as not to be overwhelming. If you're looking for a rock solid, all-in-one dashboard, you can't go wrong with SproutSocial.

- **Webfluenz**—This is a social media management platform that allows you to monitor, analyze, engage, and generally run your entire social media campaign from one place. You can check visitor demographics, geographic coverage, and a whole slew of other items. Webfluenz is especially well suited for companies that have a large, global presence.

A wide variety of tools are available to help you track prospect and customer data. But Google Analytics, KISSmetrics, SproutSocial, and Webfluenz are the top tools in this category—you won't go wrong with any of them.

Measuring Traffic on Your Competitors' Websites

You're probably interested in measuring the traffic to your website because it gives you insights into your target market's behavior. Similarly, you should be interested in measuring the traffic to your competitors' websites because it gives you insights into their prospects and customers. Both metrics are important but different.

One of the best tools to measure visits to a competitor's blog is Compete.com. The Freemium version is an engaging and powerful tool that lets you check traffic data on competing websites. (It's worth noting that Compete.com doesn't track all websites—just sites with a reasonable amount of traffic.) Compete.com also lets you compare traffic across a variety of websites. So, for example, you could compare the unique monthly visits to AcmePlumbing.com, ZZZPlumbing.com, and AAAPlumbing.com all at once.

Alexa.com is another good tool for measuring traffic. It usually focuses on the very largest websites, but it has a number of good features that can come in handy for people interested in measuring the chatter around a specific website. Some of these features include the capability to look at traffic statistics, audience information, traffic rank, page views, reach, and bounce rate.

Measuring Traffic on Your Social Media Channels

Where do most of your YouTube viewers live? What are the demographics of your Facebook fans? And how many people in your Linked In group went to Yale? These are just some of the insights you can derive simply by taking a deeper dive into the tools readily available to you—for free, no less—on your existing social media channels.

Next time you're uploading a video to your YouTube channel, go to the My Account link and navigate to your YouTube Insights page. There you'll uncover a wealth of information about your visitors. You'll be able to find out the ages of the people who are looking at your videos, how many are male or female, and the total number of views your videos are getting. You'll even be able to see how *attentive people were when they were watching your videos.* Seriously, YouTube has analytics tools that can tell whether people are doing other activities (such as checking e-mails) while watching your videos. It's scary. And kind of cool. Come to think of it, it's both scary and cool all wrapped up into one.

Facebook has a similar set of tools. Facebook Insights can provide information about your total number of fans, their interactions with the page, and the number of wall posts they've made. It can also provide demographic information such as age and gender. And you can manipulate all of this data on easy-to-use, graphical charts that can quickly give you a snapshot of your visitors and their interactions with your Facebook page.

LinkedIn provides some good information about your connections, but it focuses more on individuals than broad swaths of people. For example, you can find out where one of your connections went to college, where that person worked, and whether he already knows some of the people you know. LinkedIn is perfect for people in sales who need to get the inside scoop on someone before smiling and dialing.

Other tools are coming online all the time. Some of these tools are designed to give you insights into your visitors and followers on Twitter, Flickr, Vimeo, and other sites, so keep an eye out for them. Most of all, *use them*. There's no point in having access to information unless you're going to derive insights from your data.

Measuring Your Online Mentions across Different Platforms

Are you interested in finding out what people are saying about your brand across blogs, microblogs, message boards, wikis, and video-sharing sites? That's not as difficult as it once was. Today, tools such Social Mention, Spiral16, Google Alerts, and BrandsEye can help you do that.

Here's a quick rundown of these tools:

- **Social Mention**—This simple web-based application lets you search popular channels such as blogs and microblogs to find brand mentions and analyzes the sentiment toward your brand. You can also set up alerts so that you will be told any time someone mentions your brand.

- **BrandsEye**—A slightly different type of social media listening tool, BrandsEye helps you manage your online reputation by finding all of your brand mentions, the reputation of their source, and the sentiment. It even flags mentions that may require your immediate attention.

- **Oracle Social**—This software goes beyond monitoring what is being said about your brand online, and analyzes specific posts and snippets of posts to get the true sentiment surrounding your brand. Additionally, it identifies who the influencers are for your brand. Oracle Social is best suited for large, enterprise-sized clients.

- **Spiral16**—If you're a visual person, Spiral16 may be just what you're looking for. It's a web-based platform that helps you listen, measure, and visualize your brand's online presence. You can measure the impact your traditional campaigns have on your social media campaigns and understand why consumers are behaving the way they are. It's a data-centric platform that uses graphics to quickly and efficiently help you spot trends and react to them in real time.

- **Google Alerts**—If you're not already using Google Alerts, put down the book and go to Google.com/alerts to set it up. It takes about two minutes to type in several keywords and then get daily e-mails letting you know what was said about those keywords and where. For example, you'll want to set up your Google Alerts to tell you when someone has mentioned your brand or your competitors' brands online. You can even set it up to alert you to topical mentions such as "marketing tips" or *How to Make Money with Social Media.*

Other Quantitative Metrics

You'll want to keep track of other important metrics as you grow your social media campaign. Here's a quick rundown of some of them:

- Social bookmarks
- Inbound links to your website
- Click-throughs on your website
- Likes/Favorites on Facebook
- E-book downloads
- User-initiated reviews
- Ratings
- Traffic generated by earned media vs. free media
- Participation in polls
- Contest entries
- New e-newsletter subscribers
- E-newsletter unsubscribers

By breaking down your data into these distinct categories, you'll be able to develop key insights around each set of data:

- Traffic on your own website

- Traffic on your competitors' sites

- Traffic on the social media channels you own

- Comments about your brand, your competitors' brands, or other topics on social media channels you don't own

- Inbound links, ratings, e-book downloads, and other relevant metrics

The bottom line is that social media provides a wealth of information for anyone who wants to spend a few minutes tracking it down. The problem isn't a lack of data; the problem is that there's *too much data*. By breaking down your data into several distinct categories, it's easier to wrap your mind around it and keep track of the insights derived from it.

With that in mind, let's recap some of the key concepts and action steps from this chapter:

- **Key concept**—You can measure a wide range of quantitative data on your social media campaign, including traffic to your site, traffic to your competitors' sites, and traffic on social media channels you own.

- **Action step**—Break down your data into groups so that you can wrap your mind around the information and develop insights from it.

- **Key concept**—You can track comments about your brand, your competitors' brands, and your industry by using a few simple tools, such as BrandsEye, Spiral16, Google Alerts, and Social Mention.

- **Action step**—Don't use all of these tools, or you'll be overwhelmed. Your best bet is to start with Google Alerts and then add one other tool on top of that.

- **Key concept**—Some important quantitative metrics fall outside the groups we've broken out here. They include e-book downloads, inbound links to your website, user-generated ratings, and other data.

- **Action step**—Figure out three to six additional metrics you'd like to keep track of. Even though these metrics fall outside of the nice, tidy little groupings we've created, it doesn't mean that they aren't important. You should still keep tabs on them.

Endnote

1. https://support.google.com/analytics/answer/2525491?hl=en; http://gigaom.com/2010/03/17/sequoias-kvamme-social-media-marketing-can-replace-advertising/

22

Measuring the Qualitative Data

In the previous chapter, we discussed some of the tools and techniques you need to make quantitative measurements in your social media campaign. These include things such as the number of Twitter followers, the number of website comments, and even the bounce rate on your website.

ll these are important metrics, but they're just the first step to getting an in-depth and complete understanding of the effectiveness of your campaign. Quantitative data is important, but so is *qualitative* data.

What is qualitative data? It's the data that gives you an understanding of the emotions, thoughts, or feelings people have surrounding your products and services. You can gain a lot of insight into your brand and how people perceive it by studying what people are saying about it online. Previously, we mentioned that if people say your product is "inexpensive," it has a much different meaning than if they say it is "cheap." And if someone said your YouTube video was "funny," that would be much better than if they said it was "laughable."

You can get qualitative data about your social media campaign in two primary ways. The first is to use tools readily available on the Internet to "listen in" on people's public conversations about your brand online. The second is to ask people directly by using inbound and outbound surveys.

Let's start by talking about inbound and outbound surveys. As you know, a survey is a tool you can use to get data and insights into people's impressions of your brand. With an inbound survey, prospects and customers have come to you and stumbled upon a survey tool or button on your site. With an outbound survey, you've reached out to prospects and customers and asked them to participate in your survey.

DID YOU KNOW?

Most people fall into the trap of measuring just the *quantitative* data about their campaign, but the deepest insights are often found in the *qualitative* data.

Three popular tools for inbound surveys on your blog or website are UserVoice, Kampyle, and Get Satisfaction. You may have seen these tools on a few blogs or websites you've visited. Typically, they include a tab or button located on the site that, once clicked, provides a short survey or forum for visitors to provide useful feedback.

Here's a quick rundown of each platform:

- **UserVoice** is easy to install and is perfect for organizations where customer service is important. Over 160,000 organizations have used UserVoice, and it was the first company to provide the embeddable "Feedback" tab that's seen on many websites. User-Voice has a helpdesk function so you can provide online customer service to your web visitors.

- **Kampyle** allows you to drop a line of code into your website that places a Feedback tab on one of the corners of your site. Visitors see the feedback form and can provide short suggestions, compliments, or input on their experience with your brand, website, or blog.

- **Get Satisfaction** allows feedback from prospects and customers across a variety of other venues, including Facebook and Word-Press websites. Users can ask a question, share an idea, report a problem, or give praise. You also get the ability to respond to their input.

You can expand the scope of your inbound survey by creating an entire website designed to generate feedback. As discussed earlier, Starbucks has done this with the MyStarbucksIdea.com website. It gives people an opportunity to share their ideas for improving Starbucks with others, and can then vote on their favorites, discuss which ones they like the best, and see the results of their feedback. It's a robust website with great links and pages—definitely worth checking out.

Outbound surveys are surveys that you create and send to customers and prospects. The best and easiest way to send out an outbound survey is via e-mail, using a tool such as FluidSurveys, SurveyMonkey, or iContact. In most cases, you'll direct the e-mail recipient to a web page that includes the survey where you can track and analyze your results.

Creating Your Own Survey

What are some questions you might want to ask in an inbound and outbound survey? How should you write the questions? And what can you learn from someone who didn't buy your product or service?

Consider a few tips on creating a survey, to help you get started:

- Introduce only one issue for every question. If the issue is complex, divide it into several questions.

- Make sure your questions are crisp and clear. Test them on business associates first, to ensure that there's no room for misinterpretation.

- Are you interested in finding out whether your customers are satisfied? Some customer satisfaction questions include "How satisfied were you with your purchase?" and "How satisfied were you with your customer service?" and "How satisfied were you with our company overall?"

- Are you interested in finding out whether your customers are loyal? Some customer loyalty questions include "How likely are you to buy from us again?" and "How likely are you to recommend our product/service to others?" and "How likely are you to recommend our company to others?"

Remember, surveys aren't just about information; they're about insights. What trends have you spotted? Do they vary by region? What are the demographics of the people responding to your survey? What unspoken insights can you derive from the data? Don't just look at the data—try to draw actionable insights from it.

You'll learn more from a lost prospect than from a gained customer. If you can contact prospects who didn't buy your product or service, ask them why they didn't buy it. Find out if they can articulate what drove them away. Sometimes the answers will surprise you: "I didn't like your logo." Other times, the answers will frustrate you: "Your salesperson didn't return my call."

Listening to the Online Conversation

We have some good news. When someone makes a comment about your brand on a blog post, a forum, a Twitter account, a Facebook page, or just about any other social media platform, that's public information. It's as if they stood on a street corner with a megaphone and announced to the world that they're a fan (or not) of your product or service.

We have some better news. Plenty of wonderful tools are available for monitoring those conversations. Some of them are free. The best ones cost money. But if you're a company that's interested in getting insights into your customers and prospects, these tools are a great way to do that.

But wait—it gets even better. Some of these tools actually do some of the work for you. After all, if you downloaded a slew of comments about your brand, you'd be overwhelmed pretty quickly. The best tools allow you to derive insights into the sentiment associated with comments about your brand. That way, you can get a deeper understanding about people's thoughts and feelings about your brand.

THE BIG IDEA

Quantitative data gives you a snapshot of the state of your social media campaign. **Qualitative** data provides you deeper insights about your customers' needs and wants.

We discussed several tools in the previous chapter that help measure the quantitative data surrounding your social media campaign. Some of those tools can also measure the qualitative data surrounding your social media conversation. In other words, they can give you insights into the meaning behind the conversations.

Here's a quick rundown on some of the most important tools on that front:

- **Social Radar**—This tool enables you to track, measure, analyze, and understand chatter from all over the Web. You can track a new product launch, measure the response of an ad campaign, listen to the thoughts and opinions of consumers, analyze buzz, and review where to target your ads and social efforts. You can even measure and track mentions of any topic during any time range, dating back several years. Best of all, you can measure the sentiment of conversations and learn what's causing the emotions behind the comments.

- **Socialbakers**—This analytics platform is perfect if you're looking for in-depth data that allows you to measure, compare, and contrast your campaigns against your competitors. They have reams of data available for free on their website and specialize in global analytics. Twenty percent of the Global Fortune 500 use Socialbakers.

- **Vocus**—This is an all-encompassing online marketing tool that includes a lot of bells and whistles. If your needs go beyond just social listening and you're looking for a more robust online management tool (including PR), this is a rock-solid platform that delivers the goods.

- **CrowdBooster**—If you like data presented in easy-to-digest graphics, then you'll want to check out CrowdBooster. You can review the number of replies, impressions, Likes, comments, and other metrics in real time so you can quickly adapt to your audience's reaction.

- **SproutSocial**—We've mentioned SproutSocial a few times already because it has a really excellent platform. When it comes to monitoring the qualitative data around your social media campaign, SproutSocial delivers the goods.

- **Spiral16**—This tool can help you listen, measure, and visualize your brand's online presence. You can even measure the impact your traditional campaigns have on your social media campaigns and understand why customers are behaving the way they are.

- **Oracle Social**—This is a cloud service that helps you manage and scale your relationships with customers and social media channels. It includes social listening, social engagement, social publishing, social content, and social analytics. It's not inexpensive, but it has all the bells and whistles. It's especially good for large, enterprise-sized businesses.

- **Rapleaf**—With Rapleaf, you reverse-append existing data, such as e-mail addresses, to match social media profiles. In other words, you can use your e-mail database and, based on existing profiles on LinkedIn, Facebook, and other social media platforms, derive insights into the wants, needs, and desires of your existing pool of customers and prospects. It's not a classic social brand monitoring tool, but it can be very effective if you have an existing database.

That should give you a quick snapshot of some of the better tools available to measure the qualitative nature of your social media campaign. New tools are coming online all the time, so don't hesitate to do a search on "social media monitoring tools" or "how to measure online sentiment."

Mistakes to Avoid When Measuring Qualitative Social Media Data

People do three things wrong when they set up a qualitative social media measurement program. By keeping these three on your radar screen, you can avoid shooting yourself in the foot:

- **Gathering too much data**—It's tempting to gather reams of data about your social media campaign, but a better solution is to start small, with just a few sets of data. Wrap your mind around those and watch for trends. When you've got a handle on those sets of data, add one or two more. Rinse and repeat.

- **Not sharing the data**—If you're in marketing, you'll be looking at the data with a different set of eyes than someone in sales. Ditto for someone in the C-level suite. Remember that sharing data isn't about spewing spreadsheets around the office. It's about providing data along with insights about that data. When you share insights, you're allowing others to build upon your initial input. That's good for you and your company.

- **Not acting upon the data**—This is another all-too-common problem. People forget that data is just data until you do something with it. If you're presenting a report, be sure you end the report with action steps based on the data.

With that said, let's talk about the key concepts and action steps from this chapter:

- **Key concept**—You can use two kinds of social media surveys to gather actionable data from customers and prospects: inbound and outbound.

- **Action step**—Decide which kind of survey is best for your purposes. In some cases, you want to incorporate both inbound and outbound surveys to get the best results.

- **Key concept**—A number of good tools enable you to monitor the social media chatter about your company online.

- **Action step**—Use one of the tools to gather data. But use your most important tool, your brain, to derive insights from the data.

- **Key concept**—The three most common mistakes to avoid when monitoring social media qualitative data are 1) gathering too much data, 2) not sharing the data, and 3) not acting upon the data.

- **Action step**—Of these three, the most egregious crime is not acting upon the data. What's the point of gathering data if you're not going to act upon it?

23

All Roads in Social Media
Should Lead to ROI

We've talked about where marketing has been and where it's going. Now it's time to talk about something that's important right now: your return on investment (ROI). After all, the only real reason you're setting up, running, and managing a social media campaign is to make money, right?

Before we dive into ROI, let's talk about an important concept called **customer lifetime value (CLV)**, which is the amount of revenue you'll generate from one customer during the lifetime of your relationship.

For example, let's assume you're a cable TV provider who knows that the average customer spends $100 a month on your service. In 12 months, you generate $1,200 from the typical customer. But that customer doesn't stay with you for just 12 months. He stays with you for 3.5 years, which means that his customer lifetime value is $4,200 ($100 per month × 12 months × 3.5 years).

The next step is to figure out how much money you'd spend to acquire that customer. Many chief marketing officers (and chief financial officers) believe that 10 percent of CLV is a good estimate. So in the example of the cable company, you might spend approximately $420 in marketing costs to gain a new customer. That's considered your allowable **cost per acquisition (CPA)**, which is sometimes called **cost per sale (CPS)**.

Many companies spend a lot of time analyzing their CLV and their CPA. On the low end of the scale, you might have a software company that sells its software for $49. Its customers might purchase the software only once every two years, and they might repurchase it only when it contains a significant upgrade. In this example, the company's CLV is just $49 (because customers repurchase only when the product contains a significant upgrade), which leaves *just $4.90 for the company's allowable CPA.*

On the other end of the spectrum might be a car company that sells a model for $40,000. If the average customer buys 2.5 cars from the car company before switching brands, that's a CLV of $100,000 and an allowable CPA of $10,000—not bad.

The bottom line is that you can use multiple approaches to calculate CLV and CPA. The examples mentioned previously start you with a good, basic formula for understanding the metrics of your social media ROI.

Using Social Media for Customer Retention Purposes

A general rule of thumb for most businesses is that *it costs three to five times as much to get a new customer as it does to keep an existing one.* That's part of the reason most corporations focus so much time and money on customer retention—it pays to keep existing customers happy.

For example, say you're The Home Depot and there's a Lowe's across the street from you. (This is not as unusual as you might think.) You'd probably spend a great deal of money training your employees on everything they need to know about customer retention. If it costs three to five times as much to acquire a new customer as it does to prevent an existing one from leaving, it would be smart to focus time and money on keeping the existing customer satisfied.

Another great example of this is the Comcast cable company. It has a number of formidable competitors, ranging from AT&T to DirecTV. Comcast, AT&T, and DirecTV all know their CLV and their CPA. And they spend a lot of money training their customer service representatives on how to keep and maintain their existing customers.

That's exactly what was crossing Frank Eliason's mind when he was taking a spin around Twitter one day and noticed that some of Comcast's existing customers were venting their frustrations about Comcast on Twitter. As a longstanding employee of Comcast, the odds were pretty good that Eliason knew Comcast's CLV and that he also understood how hard it is for any corporation to get new customers. So when Eliason saw people venting their frustrations with Comcast on Twitter, it hit pretty close to home.

The good news (for Eliason, anyway) is that he knew he could solve a lot of the customers' issues remotely. For example, when a customer loses Internet connection, the solution is often to turn off the modem and then turn it back on again. Half the people tweeting their frustrations were complaining about their Internet connection, and Eliason realized that he could fix the problem via Twitter (for example, "Hey, @60SecondTweets—if you're having problems with your connection, turn off your modem and then turn it back on again. If that doesn't work, call us at 1-800-COMCAST.").

Let's assume that Comcast's CLV is the $4,200 that we mentioned in the previous cable example. (That's a guess, but it's probably not far off.) The allowable CPA in that calculation is $420. If it costs three to five times as much to get a new customer as it does to keep an existing one, then Eliason knows that every time he prevents a customer from leaving Comcast to go to DirecTV, he's saving his company between $1,260 and $2,100.

Now before you run to your CFO with these figures, you should note a few things. First, we don't know for sure that Comcast's CLV is $4,200. Second, the cost to get a new customer varies by industry, so the three to five times figure might be different for your company. Third, not everyone who complains on Twitter about Comcast goes to a competitor. (In fact, only a small percentage do.) However, these metrics *can* give you an idea of how to create a model to calculate the ROI of one aspect of your social media program.

Generating Leads with Social Media

Many companies sell their products over the Internet on e-commerce sites. It works successfully for 1-800-Flowers, iTunes, and Over Stock.com. But what if you don't sell products online? What if you're Roto-Rooter, a car dealership, or a real estate agent? If you're in one of these businesses, you're interested in generating *leads*.

A **lead** is an inbound prospect who is interested in your product or service (or your competitor's product or service). If you can capture a lead and nurture it through the sales funnel, you can convert that prospect into a customer. And that means revenue for your company.

The challenge many people face when they use social media to generate leads is that they don't go the final mile. They use social media to build awareness and generate demand for their products or services, but they don't know how to take the final step and turn it into a viable lead.

One of the best ways to use social media to generate leads is to become an *information station* for people in your target market. That's what BKV Digital and Direct Response did with the 60 Second Marketer.

As we've mentioned, BKV is a marketing communications firm that develops highly measurable marketing programs for corporations such as AT&T, Six Flags, and the American Red Cross. The idea for the 60 Second Marketer started with an analysis of BKV's target market, which is composed of marketing directors working at large corporations throughout the world.

If you get inside the mind of the typical marketing director at these corporations, you find someone who is very busy and interested in staying abreast of the latest tools, tips, and techniques in marketing. BKV estimated that marketing directors download two to three marketing white papers a month, but they have time to read only a couple of pages of those white papers. The rest get stacked on their desk—unread—and then get tossed in the trash about once every three months.

But what if you could distill those white papers to their essence? What if you could put the most important information into a short, 60-second video that gave the marketing director the key bits of information about the new tool, tip, or technique?

BKV did that with the 60 Second Marketer. BKV set it up to be an information station for marketing directors and, in the process, to introduce them to BKV Digital and Direct Response. BKV nurtured the leads captured through the 60 Second Marketer until the company could convert them into clients through the sales funnel.

The 60 Second Marketer uses a hub-and-spoke system to drive prospects to the website and to capture their attention. When prospects sign up for the e-newsletter, participate in a free Webinar, or attend a 60 Second Marketer event, they get subtle, long-term exposure to BKV. The result is an engaged and loyal prospect base, some of whom convert to customers.

You can do the same with your social media campaign. As soon as you've finished this chapter (and not a moment before), we recommend that you sketch out a hub-and-spoke system of your own and use it as a way to analyze which social media tools you will use to capture lead data for your business.

Converting Leads into Customers

What should you do when you've captured the lead data for your customer prospects? You should start remarketing to them to close the loop. A lead is just a lead until you actively pursue it and convert it to a customer.

This requires good, old-fashioned hard work. Your parents and grandparents used a telephone to connect with prospects for their businesses. They also used sales letters. E-mail is another good tool to convert prospects into customers. The only difference is that your grandparents (and, perhaps, your parents) didn't use it.

A lead doesn't count for anything until you do the hard work to convert it to a sale. That's the final mile, and it's probably the hardest mile. But executing that last mile differentiates the social media wannabes from the social media superstars.

Tracking Your Social Media ROI

In Chapter 20, "How to Measure the Impact of Your Social Media Campaign," we mentioned that the only truly important social media metric is ROI. Everything else—traffic, comments, followers, leads—is just a stop along the way.

In this chapter, we've covered a lot of important concepts, including CLV, CPA, lead generation, and prospect conversion. If you understand those concepts, the rest is just a matter of tracking the data and using it to improve your results.

Most people are familiar with an old question: If a tree falls in the woods and nobody is there to hear it fall, does it still make a sound? The same question holds true for social media: If a social media campaign isn't measured, is it effective? The answer is "no." A social media campaign that isn't measured isn't effective because you can't tell whether it worked.

The specifics of measuring a social media campaign vary with every company, but let's use a basic example to illustrate the approach. Let's say that you're a lawn care company, and your typical customer spends $80 per month on your service and stays with you for three years. That gives you a CLV of $2,880 and an allowable CPA of $288.

In the past, you might have used direct mail as your primary tool to generate leads and convert those leads into sales. If the conversion rate on your direct mail campaigns was 0.5 percent, you'd have to send out 200 direct mail pieces to acquire a customer. If your printing, postage, list, and marketing costs for those direct mail pieces was $1.44 each, the math works out perfectly to $288. You're golden.

But let's say that the CEO and CFO decide to test a social media campaign against the existing direct mail campaign. Now the math gets kind of interesting. Let's assume that you spend $2.4 million each year to send out two million direct mail pieces that generate 10,000 new customers each year (2 million direct mail pieces × 0.5% = 10,000 new customers). If your annual revenue per customer is $960, that's $9.6 million in incremental revenue each year from new customers. (Don't forget that you have some customer churn, so some of the $9.6 million replaces revenue from lost customers.)

You want to test your social media campaign against your direct mail campaign. If you spend $2.4 million each year on your direct mail campaign, a safe bet would be to spend 10 percent of that, or $240,000, on a "test social media" campaign.

The costs associated with setting up, launching, and running a social media campaign are often underestimated. Because you don't have media costs for using Twitter, YouTube, Facebook, LinkedIn, or other social media platforms, people often assume that running a social media campaign is cheap. But the manpower involved in running a social media campaign can be significant. So can the costs for producing the content for your social media campaign.

If you're a large company with a brand to protect, you need to create top-notch landing pages on your website. That costs money. So do well-produced YouTube videos and effective Facebook promotions.

The point is, you need to dive deep into some of the hidden costs of social media to get a good, clear understanding of your campaign's ROI. In this example, we said that you have $240,000 to spend on labor and production costs. For that $240,000 investment to match the ROI of the direct mail campaign, it would have to generate 1,000 new customers.

That's not as easy as it looks, but it's also not impossible. One of your objectives might be to drive 100,000 people to your landing pages via your social media campaign. Assuming that you were able to do that, it's reasonable to calculate that 1,000 of those would convert to customers, which would match your direct mail campaign dollar for dollar. From that point on, it's simply a matter of testing ways to grow your inbound traffic and to improve your conversion rate.

The Bottom Line

The most important thing you can do is track your campaign to the level of prospect conversion. When you're tracking data at that level, you can calculate your ROI. And assuming that the ROI is positive, you can grow your campaign and improve efficiencies over time. And that, friends, translates into profits.

- **Key concept**—Customer lifetime value (CLV) is the revenue you'll generate from a typical customer during the lifetime of your engagement.

- **Action step**—Calculate your CLV using this simple formula: monthly revenue × 12 months × average customer life cycle = CLV.

- **Key concept**—Allowable cost per acquisition (CPA) is the amount of money you would spend to acquire a new customer.

- **Action step**—Determine your allowable CPA by calculating 10 percent of your CLV.

- **Key concept**—Leads and prospects generate $0 for your company until you convert them into customers.

- **Action step**—Embrace the idea that a social media campaign is useless unless you convert your leads and prospects into customers. Track your data to the prospect conversion level, to generate a clear sense of your actual ROI.

24

How to Ensure Your Social Media Campaign Runs Smoothly

If you're a real estate agent, an interior designer, or a landscape company, making the decision to set up, run, and manage a social media campaign can be pretty simple. Only a handful of people have to buy into the concept, and with a little planning and strategizing, you can be off to the races pretty quickly.

But if you work at a larger corporation, getting buy-in is only part of the challenge. Invariably, you'll be asked to set up a series of *social media guidelines* for the 10 or 100 or 1,000 people who are going to be helping you execute your program.

Remember, as our friend Erik Qualman states in his book *Socialnomics*, "What happens in Vegas, stays on YouTube." With that in mind, the last thing your corporation wants is for a random comment or inappropriate conversation to make its way across the social media sphere. It's the quickest way we know to dampen the effects of a successful social media campaign. But at the same time, it's important to recognize that the snowball effect of social media can really work only when employees are given the freedom to respond openly and quickly on any of your social media channels.

Let's take a look at five core values that we've compiled as guiding principles for your company's social media program. These values are based on research we've done into the ways companies such as Dell and The Coca-Cola Company conduct their social media campaigns.

The Five Core Values of Social Media Behavior

All employees who are asked to participate in social media dialogues should embrace the following core values:

- **Show respect**—The people on the other end of your social media dialogue are human, too. They have feelings, emotions, and points of view just like you do. Treat them like your neighbors (or, at least, like the neighbors you're friends with).

- **Show responsibility**—Take initiative to be trustworthy. If you've been assigned to the social media team, that means you've been given a certain level of responsibility. Honor that responsibility by taking it seriously.

- **Demonstrate integrity**—Show sound, moral character. Pretend your grandmother is watching you. After all, she probably is, from somewhere.

- **Be ethical**—Be right and honest in your conduct. If you find yourself doing something that you can't be totally transparent about, it's probably not the right thing to do.

- **Add value**—Move the ball forward in all your conversations. Provide an insight, a point of view, or something helpful in each one of your interactions. Every time you move the ball forward an inch, you're helping your company achieve its goals.

Now let's drill down a bit and look at 17 guiding principles that fall under these five core values.

17 Social Media Principles for Corporations

Under each value outlined in the last section, you'll find several guiding principles that encourage your employees to be responsible in all your social media initiatives.

Show Respect

- *Respect property.* Show respect for the opinions and property of your company and of others. Give credit when appropriate, get permission when needed.

- *Respect privacy.* Any information gathered or personal identifiers collected about customers should not be published irresponsibly or misused. There are no exceptions to this rule.

- *Respect copyrights and trademarks.* Do not post another company's trademarks or any copyrighted material belonging to another company without getting approval first.

Show Responsibility

- *Accept personal responsibility.* You post it, you accept the consequences.

- *Demonstrate admirable online behavior.* Express yourself, but remember anything you say lives forever on the Internet. Comply with any regulations that govern your site.

- *Conscientiously represent your company.* Everything you say as a member of the company represents the company. Likewise, writing harshly about your company can have repercussions for you, obviously, when your company gets the news. If internal issues arise within your business, keep them internal.

- *Mix personal and business lives carefully.* Remember, everything you post on your personal Facebook or MySpace could get back to the company.

Demonstrate Integrity

- *Show transparency.* If you work for a company, you should reveal that information when commenting about that company or its competition.

- *Use good judgment.* Share your opinions online, but avoid anything that could be considered poor taste; it reflects poorly on you and your company. Certainly avoid anything that could be considered illegal.

- *Provide a framework for your arguments.* Provide background to support your postings. Arguments that are thoughtful and that go beyond "xx sucks" make your point of view more valid.

Be Ethical

- *Protect the company's proprietary information.* You are obligated by your contract to protect vital company information, and state laws govern trade secrets.

- *Don't forget your day job.* It's important to maintain productivity at your job and not get lost in cyberspace. Realize that customer service may best be handled through social media, but avoiding your work to post an opinion about the new company dress code doesn't add value.

- *Let the experts be the experts.* Your readers may have questions on specific products or services about which you have limited knowledge. Forward those questions for the experts to respond to. The same holds true for PR issues.

- *Post truthful information.* Do your research to ensure that you aren't just spreading rumors. Correct errors if you find them later.

Add Value

- *Provide value for customers.* Social media should bring customers closer to the products and services you sell. Ranting on Facebook about the way the shipping department messes everything up makes you look petty and provides no value for the customers. The same holds true for not responding to customers' comments.

- *Monitor your social media sites.* Posting to a Facebook page and then not monitoring it defeats the purpose and is not social media participation. Online sources must be nurtured though active monitoring and participation.

- *Remember the audience.* Don't forget that readers include clients—past, present, and future—and employees. Don't publish anything that would insult or otherwise alienate these people.

Put These Guidelines in Place Sooner Rather than Later

The Internet is rife with stories from companies or individuals who wish they'd followed these guidelines. One of the more notable is Domino's Pizza, a company that spends tens of millions of dollars each year building and nurturing its brand.

Unfortunately, several rogue employees at a Domino's franchise in North Carolina decided to post a prank YouTube video of some unsanitary and disgusting food-preparation practices. The viral nature of the Internet helped the video generate a million views within days of being uploaded. Worse still, for a short while, Google had five different links on its first page highlighting the video.

It's unfortunate that a few irresponsible employees at a small franchise can do so much damage to a business that has spent so much time and money building a deservedly good reputation. But social media doesn't care how many years you've spent building a brand, even when what's posted on YouTube is false.

Domino's isn't the only company that has had to deal with these kinds of challenges. Not long ago, an employee of a large, well-respected public relations firm was flying to Memphis, Tennessee, to discuss, of all things, *social media* with one of the firm's largest clients, FedEx. Unfortunately, this employee, who, as a social media expert, should have known better, decided to tweet his disdain for the city of Memphis just as he was exiting the city's airport.

Twenty minutes later, as he was entering the FedEx headquarters, all hell had broken loose. A number of FedEx employees who followed this gentleman on Twitter saw his tweet about Memphis and, as proud residents of said city, took offense.

Within days, the story had spread across the globe, embarrassing the employee and the PR agency, and bringing into question FedEx's wisdom for hiring a social media expert who assumed nobody was reading his tweets.

Of course, it's easy to look back on other people's missteps and to use 20/20 hindsight to critique their actions and responses. That's actually not our intent with these stories. Our intent is to use these illustrations to highlight the importance of putting some social media guidelines in place as you roll out your social media program.

Let's take a look at some of the key concepts and action steps from this chapter before we move on to the next chapter for a step-by-step action plan for a social media campaign:

- **Key concept**—As Erik Qualman says, "What happens in Vegas, stays on YouTube."

- **Action step**—Help employees understand that once a comment, video, or dialogue is posted on the Internet, it's very hard, if not impossible, to make it disappear.

- **Key concept**—All employees should follow five core values and 17 principles if they're going to participate in a corporate social media campaign.

- **Action step**—Review the five core values and 17 principles with all the employees who will be part of the social media team. It sounds like a goofy thing to do, but it'll help them understand that you're taking this seriously.

- **Key concept**—Companies such as Domino's and FedEx have had their share of negative experiences with social media.

- **Action step**—If it can happen to Domino's and FedEx, it can happen to you. Be proactive and incorporate these guidelines into your corporate DNA today.

25

A Step-by-Step Action Plan
for Social Media Success

We've covered a lot of important information in the past few hundred pages. You might have jotted down a few notes in the margins, or you might have reviewed and taken action on some of the key concepts and action steps at the end of every chapter. But sometimes it helps to have a single chapter with a long checklist of tasks you'll need to perform in order to have a successful social media campaign.

That's what this chapter is for. It doesn't cover every task we've discussed in the previous chapters, but it should give you a starting point from which you can launch your campaign.

So here goes. Put a check mark next to each task as you complete it. Before you know it, you'll be well on your way to generating real money from your social media campaign.

What follows are the preliminaries:

- I've conducted a review of my company's *business* and understand its mission, goals, and objectives.

- I've conducted a review of my company's *sales program* and understand how a prospect is brought into the sales funnel and converted into a customer.

- I've conducted a review of my company's *marketing program* and understand the role the marketing program plays in the overall success of the company.

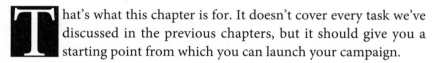

- I've conducted a review of the strategies, tactics, and tools involved in a social media campaign and understand the role each of those strategies, tactics, and tools plays in a well-run social media program.

- After doing all of this, I've asked myself, "Do I genuinely understand how a prospect arrives into our sales funnel and how we can nurture that prospect until he or she becomes a customer?" If I've concluded that I understand this, I can move on to the next steps.

Next, move on to a review of the competitive landscape:

- I've reviewed the *overall strengths and weaknesses* of my company's top five competitors.

- I've reviewed the *sales and marketing* efforts of my top five competitors.

- I've analyzed the specific *social media campaigns* being conducted by my top five competitors.

- I've created a list of social media strategies and tactics my competitors are using that appear to be *effective.*

- I've created a list of social media strategies and tactics my competitors are using that appear to be *ineffective.*

- I've joined my competitors' LinkedIn groups, Facebook pages, YouTube channels, Twitter accounts, and other social media member sites.

- I've set up Google Alerts to send me notifications any time my competitors, my industry, or my company is mentioned in blogs or articles online.

Then engage with your internal management team:

- I've asked the social media proponents in my organization to be advocates for my program. I've asked them to be engaged in any way they can to help my social media program succeed.

- I've identified people within my organization who might not be social media advocates and have begun a program to help them understand the value a well-run social media program can bring to our company.

- I've assembled a team to help me set up, run, and manage the social media program for my company.

- I've suggested that each team member become familiar with *How to Make Money with Social Media* to ensure that we're all working from the same playbook.

- I've asked each team member to join the e-newsletter lists for the top social media blogs, including SocialMediaExaminer.com, SocialMediaToday.com, and 60SecondMarketer.com.

Next, you can set yourself up for success:

- I've assembled a social media team to help me execute my program. (This team can be as small as one person or as large as 100 or more.)

- I've set specific, measurable, actionable, realistic, and time-bound goals (SMART goals) for my social media campaign.

- I've reviewed my SMART goals with my team and encouraged feedback and input.

- I've done an in-depth analysis of my target market and have a genuine understanding of who they are and what makes them tick.

- I've set up my social media campaign so that it can be measured.

- I've conducted a review of each of the three categories of social media platforms—networking platforms, promotion platforms, and sharing platforms.

- I've developed a *strategic framework* for my social media campaign that will help me accomplish my overall business goals.

- I've developed a tactical framework for my social media campaign that will help me accomplish my strategic goals.

- I've developed an executional framework for my social media program that will help me accomplish my tactical goals.

- I've aligned my social media campaign with my overall branding campaign so that they're essentially one and the same.

The days before you launch or relaunch your social media campaign:

- In an effort to get going quickly, I've completed the following tasks:
  - I've updated my company's LinkedIn page, updated our Facebook page, set up a Twitter account, created a Pinterest page, created a Google+ page, and launched any other social media channels *that are relevant to my customer base.* (Don't over-do it here. Only launch social media channels that are relevant to your customers.)
  - I've incorporated a blog into the company's website.
  - I've created a YouTube channel.
  - I've created an e-newsletter for my customers and prospects using AWeber, Constant Contact, iContact, or any of the other e-mail service providers.
  - I've updated any references our company has on Wikipedia.
  - I've uploaded content to SlideShare, Scribd, and Slideo.
  - I've added Feedback, UserVoice, or Get Statisfaction to my website.
  - I've investigated and incorporated accounts on other social media platforms, including hi5, Tumblr, Plaxo, XING, Ning, and Friendster.
- I understand that a social media campaign is an ongoing process and can't be executed in "five minutes a day." As such, I've allocated a realistic and reasonable amount of time to execute my program.

The first 30 days after launch or relaunch:

- I've committed myself to the following goals for the first 30 days of my social media campaign:
  - I'll update my company's LinkedIn profile once every two weeks with news and information about the company.

- I'll post updates to my company's Facebook page several times a day.

- I'll send out helpful, interesting tweets anywhere from 10 to 12 times a day.

- I'll write two to three blog posts a week (none of which will be about our company holiday party or our CEO's trip to the convention).

- I'll comment on five blog posts a week with a relevant, insightful comment.

- I'll upload a series of YouTube videos designed to provide value to our customers and prospects.

- I'll update my company's Google+ page with relevant posts and content that will help build awareness for my company's product or service.

- I'll upload content to SlideShare once or twice a month during the launch of the campaign.

- I'll respond to the Feedback, UserVoice, or Get Statisfaction comments left on my company's site within 24 hours of receipt.

Measuring success:

- I understand that social media can help me with customer retention and customer acquisition.

- I've installed Google Analytics, KISSmetrics, or Adobe Analytics on my company's website so that I can track inbound traffic and analyze when and how a prospect converts to a customer.

- I'm prepared to generate weekly and monthly reports that highlight the success of my social media program.

- I'm continuously *testing* my social media program so that I can improve the results and generate an increasingly robust return on investment.

How to Make Money with Social Media

There's a difference between people who make money with social media and people who don't. The people who don't make money with social media typically *never get their campaigns off the ground.* In most cases, they upload a YouTube video or update their LinkedIn profile and then claim that they have a social media campaign.

But, as we've learned in these pages, running a social media campaign is about more than just uploading a YouTube video or creating a LinkedIn profile—it's about much, much more.

The people who *do* make money with social media are different. They set objectives, create a plan, and *execute the plan relentlessly.*

You're now in a spot to make money with social media. We've given you all the best tools for a successful social media campaign and helped you understand how to implement them. The only thing we can't give you is a gentle nudge to get started, so we'd like you to nudge yourself.

Sound like a plan?

With that in mind, here are some final tips to keep you moving ahead quickly and efficiently:

- *It's better to get ten things done than it is to do one thing perfectly.* Don't get stuck trying to make everything perfect. It'll never be perfect. Besides, if you don't like your blog post, your tweet, or your LinkedIn profile, you can just go back in tomorrow and change it.

- *Begin each day with five or ten social media tasks that'll help you feel like you're off to a good start.* This is easier than you might think: Send out three tweets, answer one question on Facebook, and make one helpful comment on a good blog post you've read. See? Your day is already off to a *terrific* start.

- *Visit the 60 Second Marketer for more inspiration.* We're constantly updating the 60 Second Marketer website with content from marketing experts around the globe. Stop by and check out some of the tools, tips, and techniques we have on the site. We guarantee you'll walk away with a bunch of great marketing ideas each time you visit.

That's all, folks. Keep us posted on your progress. And let us know what tools, tips, and techniques you'd like us to incorporate into future versions of this book.

Index

I

iContact, 75
i-Cubed system, 57
  managing online conversations, 57-59
identifying
  brand essence of your company, 154-155
  competitors, 123-125
  goals for campaigns, 7, 14
IKEA, 127-128
IMC (integrated marketing communications), 117-118
impact (i-Cubed system), 57
implementing principles for corporate social media, 195-196
inbound marketing, 72-73
inbound surveys, 176-177
  creating, 177-178
increasing revenue
  with promoting platforms, 87-93
  with sharing platforms, 95-100
information (i-Cubed system), 57
InfusionSoft, 77
insight (i-Cubed system), 57
Insightly, 6
Instagram, 63, 97
integrating social media with marketing plans, 115-116, 120-121
  IMC, 117-118
  responsibility for, 119-120
internal situation analysis, conducting, 131-134
iTunes, 90

J-K

JavaBB, 88

Kampyle, 176
KISSmetrics, 23, 168

L

landing pages, 50
  driving customers to, 36
language of social media, 31
lead generation, 30
LeadLife, 77
leads
  converting into customers, 187-188
  generating with social media, 186-187
Lefora, 88
leveraging social media platforms for mobile campaigns, 110-111
life cycle of social media, 32-33
Likealyzer, 33
LinkedIn, 81
  trade show analogy, 26

M

Macy's, 132
Madison Avenue advertising agencies, 15
magnetism, 12-14, 47-48
Maid Brigade, 22
MailChimp, 75
Mamtani, Rupal, 41
management tools, 8

TripAdvisor, 111
Tumblr, 64
Turner, Jamie, 57
TweetDeck, 6, 99
tweetups, 28
Twitter, 1, 90
  cocktail party analogy, 26
  Red's Porch campaign, 11-12
  updating, 65
two-dimensional mapping scheme
  for competitive analysis, 125-127

U

understanding the customer
  decision-making process, 137
Unilever, 148
United Airlines, 17
updating
  corporate blogs, 66
  social media platforms, 65
UserVoice, 176

V

Vanilla, 88
vBulletin, 88
Vimeo, 90
Vine, 63
virtual worlds, 28
visitors
  bounce rate, 168
  converting to customers, 48, 71
  exit rate, 168
Vocus, 179
volume, measuring, 56
voting, 28

W

Webfluenz, 8, 169
websites
  Alexa.com, 170
  Compete.com, 169
  content aggregation sites, 28
  data analytics, 23
  Epicurious.com, 17
  Mention.com, 42
  photo-sharing sites, 28
  presentation-sharing sites, 28
  visitors
    converting to customers, 48
  wikis, 28
widgets, 27
Wikipedia, 64, 99
wikis, 28
WooBox, 33
word analysis, 56

X-Y-Z

XING, 82

Yahoo!, 90
Yelp, 64, 100
YouTube, 91
  monthly viewership, 27
  Times Square analogy, 27

Zagat, 111
Zoho, 88
Zuckerberg, Mark, 81
Zyman, Sergio, 137